# TROY AND HER LEGEND

Bust of Homer. National Museum, Naples

ὕψος μεγαλοφροσύνης ἀπήχημα.
Sublimity is the echo of the lofty spirit.
—Longinus. *On the Sublime*

# TROY
## AND HER
## LEGEND

BY

ARTHUR M. YOUNG

*Professor of Latin and Greek*
*University of Pittsburgh*

UNIVERSITY OF PITTSBURGH PRESS

1948

PRINTED IN THE UNITED STATES OF AMERICA

BY DAVIS & WARDE, INC., PITTSBURGH, PENNSYLVANIA

*To my students in grateful*
*remembrance of their attentive listening*

# FOREWORD

D R. YOUNG has done us a real service in essaying in this
book an ambitious project—the history of the Legend of
Troy in literature and the arts.

A friend of mine, not long ago, asked a class in Renaissance
art to describe Michelangelo's Moses. Among other bits of
useful information he learned, "Michelangelo's Moses is one
of Raphael's finest paintings of our Saviour. There he stands
with the Virgin on either side." And my friend added, "The
last time I told that story, one of the men said, 'Oh, I know that
painting. I saw it in Antwerp.'" Well, Dr. Young's book perhaps won't help to unravel the Virgin, Raphael, Moses, and
Michelangelo, but it should certainly go far toward pre-
venting any such entanglement from enmeshing Dido, Vergil,
Homer, and Priam.

For except Biblical history, no subject has been recorded in
so many artistic productions as has the Legend of Troy, and
the reader of Dr. Young's book will take notice and avoid con-
fusing Circe with Aeneas when he is confronted with a
Renaissance painting or a modern opera.

It has lately been my privilege to assist in teaching the hu-
manities to the freshmen of Scripps College. It has been a
great pleasure and an inspiration to see how the old and ever
new story of Troy catches the imagination of these girls, to
many of whom it is as fresh as it was to Nausicaa. The insult
to Achilles' honor, the love of Hector for Andromache, the
cowardice of Paris, the dignity of Priam, the timeless tragedy
of war portrayed in the *Trojan Women,* the magnificent

murderess, Clytemnestra, the steadfast goodly Odysseus, crafty Circe, jealous Calypso, wise Penelope, Nausicaa with her brave, unwavering eyes, even Aeneas momentarily humanized by passionate Dido—these are not ghosts from a dead past, but men and women, ageless and deathless, swayed with passions that are immortal. Through the warp and woof of the great tapestry of history run the purple threads of Troy.

Not long ago one of our great classical teachers said, "The men and women of the Italian Renaissance were not inspired and reborn by Greek morphology and Latin syntax, but by the content of what they read—the thoughts of Cicero, Plato, and Aristotle, the noble concept of the changeless human drama so completely expressed in the Greek and Roman poets."

For nothing seems to me so untrue as the excuse of the Emperor Lotharius, "Tempora mutantur et nos mutamur in illis." Human passions change not. "There abideth faith, hope, and love," and perhaps it is not pedantic to note that in the Greek the emphasis is on "abideth." To the Greeks it was given, beyond other peoples, to know and to depict these enduring verities. The tragedy of Hector's death and the pathos of Priam's appeal to Achilles for his dead son's body ("I have braved what none other man on earth hath braved before, to stretch forth my hand toward the face of the slayer of my sons.") move the hearts of the young people gathered at Lorenzo's court in his Florentine palace. The freshmen can as well as they

> "hear like ocean on a western beach
> The surge and thunder of the Odyssey."

It has been said that English is richer than other tongues because of our common heritage in the Bible and Shakespeare; that commonplace phrases like "green pastures" and "an honorable man" carry with them always a faint aura, a lingering glow from the great passages in which the psalmist and the poet used them. If this be true of language, it is true also in art—the great themes of the Bible and the Greek legends are an integrating and unifying influence that should be cherished in this divisive age.

I am well aware that many teachers feel that this more recent emphasis on the content and influence of the classics is a mistake, that it directs attention from the strictly scientific study of the language. I would not answer them by reminding them that it is "the letter of the law that killeth, but the spirit that maketh alive." I would rather urge them to receive as a welcome ally to our cause every book like this of Dr. Young which broadens our knowledge of classical influences—referring them to a presidential address by the great Gildersleeve (not he of the radio hour) on "Oscillations and Nutations in Philology." He was speaking of the diverse and sometimes conflicting interests of Classicists and he pleaded with the philologians and the archaeologists to adopt the liberal philosophy of the aged Jew who on his deathbed was urged to embrace the religion of Christ. The old man sighed, gathered the coverlets of his couch about him and ere he passed, replied, "The Lord our God is one God."

April, 1948

Louis E. Lord
Professor of Classical Languages and
Literature at Scripps College
Chairman of the Managing Committee of the
American School of Classical Studies at Athens

# PREFACE

IT IS the hope of the author that the readers of this book will join him in broadening the horizon of their comprehension and appreciation of the ancient classics. Those who serve as horizons to horizons will have no need for it.

The classics should be fostered today on the basis of a contemporary organic need for them in some of their varied forms. The precise area in which they can be of the greatest contemporary service can be better understood if one watches the vicissitudes of their relationships with the procession of other civilizations since their time. In the classics and their changing interrelations with later cultures an understanding of the range and capacities of the human keyboard can contribute to our intellectual maturity and emotional literacy.

Though limitations of space prescribe that this study be a survey drawing from, rather than an exhaustive treatise contributing to, the store of human knowledge—yet the overview of the classics from this new vantage point should bring to many readers a broader appreciation of their energy and value, both in and of themselves, and in solution with other cultures. Fiction which can instruct and guide to fulfillment such diverse artists and times as have gone to the legend of Troy need not blush in the presence of Reality.

For the original suggestion regarding this manuscript, I am indebted to Professor W. T. Semple of the University of Cincinnati, and for his never-failing interest and encouragement I am indebted, too. The manuscript has passed under the eyes and guiding hands of several eminent scholars who

# PREFACE

have given generously of their time and kindly wisdom to bring it to greater maturity and usefulness. I wish to acknowledge my gratitude—to name those who can be specifically mentioned—to Professors Chandler R. Post and Herbert Bloch of Harvard University, Carl W. Blegen and John L. Caskey of the University of Cincinnati, Stephen B. Luce of the Fogg Museum of Art, G. S. Dickinson of Vassar College, and to P. F. Jones and W. R. Hovey of the University of Pittsburgh for their careful reading of parts of my manuscript and helpful suggestions for its improvement. I wish also to acknowledge my gratitude to my wife for her good help with the index and to Mrs. Agnes L. Starrett, University Editor of the University of Pittsburgh, for her enthusiastic interest in bringing this manuscript through the press.

ARTHUR M. YOUNG

Pittsburgh, Pennsylvania

# CONTENTS

# CONTENTS

# ILLUSTRATIONS

# ILLUSTRATIONS

# TROY AND HER LEGEND

# I. THE LEGEND OF TROY

THE LEGEND OF TROY is the legacy of an early, heroic period in the history of Greece, a legacy gathered up long before recorded history. As it has come down in writing from classical antiquity it is a composite, verse and prose, Greek and Roman —of poet, dramatist, historian, mythographer, antiquarian, and commentator—assembled over a millennium and a half.

Its greatness through the ages depends not on any relation the story may have to historical reality—indeed, in whatever form the legend takes, it is least inspired when it pretends to be most authentic. The greatness of the Troy legend lies rather in the beauty and the variety it has called out of the creative imaginations of artists, from Homer down to modern times, artists who with varied skill and in many forms have expressed their individual genius. Through them, although in its earliest forms and setting a story of war, the legend has become the mother of the arts of peace. And, although the legend at the beginning of the Greek experience reached its most universal, complete, and inspired form in Homer, yet it had not in his day nor has it had in any period of its history a fixed official story to which interpretation must conform. In fact, when the story has been complete and consistent within itself the expression of the artist has been least vital.

The reasons for the lack of fixity of the legend in classical times are not difficult to find. Even as told in the epic fullness of Homer, the tale is far too vast in scope to be exhausted in one form or version; and the conditions under which the epic grew in early Greece did not encourage a unity of tradition.

I

Then, too, in the best of classical Greek times inventive genius and the individuality of artists were too strong to allow any freezing of the legend into mold. And, finally, the disappearance of the Greek tradition from the West for a thousand years during the Middle Ages cleared the stage of the original Greek recordings altogether and left the legend to the comforting mediocrity of re-creations of it.

Growing healthily in the minds and souls of the Greeks and Romans the legend of Troy became an amazing medium for evoking their skills and a kind of sublimating mirror of their interests and enthusiasms. It has continued so in the imaginations of the diverse brotherhood of artists who have since used it. But that it might serve us well, the legend has often had to become a humble servant. If it has become universal, it has often had to assume the garb of contemporary *mores*. In order to survive, the legend has had to submit to the pedantry of the scholar, the hesitancy of the student, and the dissecting eye of the archaeologist. It has had to cease being Greek, and at times to forego being human, but in so doing it has seemed to successive ages timely and useful. Although its manifestations vary in time and in place, the legend of Troy is universal.

For the benefit of those who are not familiar with the legend in general outline as the ancients finally left it, and to help the reader understand this book, the following summary is given. How and when and by whom the various parts of the legend were developed will appear as the story proceeds.

## GENEALOGY OF THE ROYAL TROJAN FAMILY

Dardanus, the son of Zeus, founded a colony bearing his name in the Troad, which was the region in northwestern Asia Minor, bordering the Hellespont and the Aegean Sea. His grandson was Tros, from whom the Trojans derived their name. The three sons of Tros were Ilus, Assaracus, and Ganymede. Ganymede by order of Zeus was carried off to Olympus to serve as cupbearer to the gods. From Ilus and Assaracus two diverging lines sprang, carrying with their houses a tradition of rivalry. From Ilus came in successive generations Laomedon, Priam, and Hector; and from Assaracus came Capys, Anchises, and Aeneas. Ilus founded Ilium. Hence, the words *Trojan* and *Ilium* came from two early members of the royal family in the Troad. Homer uses both Ἴλιος and Τροίη. The neuter form Ἴλιον occurs only once in Homer, but later came into common use. By the Roman poets Troia was preferred, since Ilium is not adapted for use in the dactylic hexameter. The following diagram will show at a glance the genealogy of the royal family in the Troad as we need to know it:

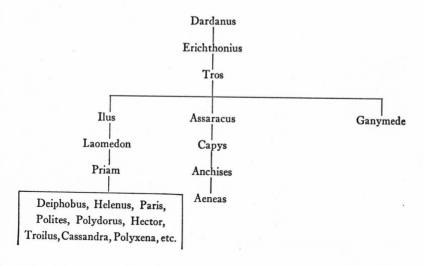

### FROM LAOMEDON TO PARIS

Under the regime of Laomedon, with the help of Poseidon and Apollo, the walls of Troy were built. But when the walls were finished, Laomedon refused to the gods the stipulated reward for their work. In retaliation Poseidon sent a monster to prey upon the land. Laomedon now promised to anyone who would rid the land of this monster those immortal steeds which Zeus had given, and was even preparing to sacrifice to the monster his own daughter, Hesione, when the arrival and intervention of Heracles saved both the land and his daughter. Says Portia of Bassanio as the latter approaches the three caskets, in *The Merchant of Venice:*

> Now he goes,
> With no less presence, but with much more love,
> Than young Alcides, when he did redeem
> The virgin tribute paid by howling Troy
> To the sea-monster.

When Laomedon, again perfidious, cheated Heracles out of his promised reward, Heracles sailed against Troy from Greece, captured Troy, and slew Laomedon and most of his family. The young Priam, however, survived and married Hecuba. In his polished halls grew up his family of fifty sons and twelve daughters. Some of his sons were Hector, Paris, Deiphobus, Helenus, Troilus, Polites, and Polydorus; of the daughters, Polyxena and Cassandra are best known. When the formidable omens attending the birth of Paris were confirmed by the pronouncement of the seers that the son about to be born would cause the destruction of Troy, Paris was exposed on Mt. Ida in the Troad. Reared by shepherds he was later recognized and adopted by his parents. He is sometimes known as Alexander. Out of his marriage with Oenone, Paris had a son, Corythus.

### THE GOLDEN APPLE AND ITS CONSEQUENCES

Meantime and while the family of Priam was growing, Zeus had decreed the Trojan War as a means of alleviating the overpopulation of the world. In this manner he provoked the war. He brought about the wedding of Peleus and Thetis in Thessaly, which readers of Catullus remember, and to the wedding came an uninvited guest, Eris, goddess of Strife. She bore, for having been so slighted, a fateful gift of vengeance— a golden apple inscribed with the words "To the most beautiful." A contest arose among the three goddesses, Athena, Hera, and Aphrodite, to determine which one of them was entitled to the award. For judgment they were referred to the shepherd, Paris, on Mt. Ida. Athena promised Paris prowess in war; Hera, broad sovereignty over men; and Aphrodite, the fairest lady in the world. This distinction was enjoyed by Helen, daughter of Zeus and of Nemesis, according to an early version. Paris awarded the prize to Aphrodite, thereby, of course, bringing down on his city, Troy, the hatred of Athena and Hera. The fulfillment of his reward Paris realized at Sparta, where he was hospitably entertained in the home of Helen and Menelaus. In the absence of Menelaus, he courted Helen and induced her to return to Troy with him. This seduction of Helen led eventually to the arrival at Troy of the Greek hosts, bent upon retaliation. For Menelaus, the husband of Helen, was the brother of Agamemnon, a powerful prince who from his strong citadel at Mycenae exercised broad sovereignty over other princes. Besides, the Greeks who had been the fellow suitors of Helen before her marriage to Menelaus had pledged themselves to avenge any harm done either to Helen or to her husband.

### GREEK EXPEDITION AND DEATH OF HECTOR

The journey of the Greek forces to Troy, however, was interrupted at Aulis by a calm sent by Artemis. That goddess expected Agamemnon to fulfill a vow once made that he would dedicate to her the fairest thing born in his land in that year, even though his baby daughter, Iphigenia, had proved to be the object of his vow. To assuage the anger of the goddess at the delay in fulfillment of the promise, the sacrifice of Iphigenia was arranged—under the pretext that she was to be married to Achilles. As the sacrificial knife was falling, however, Artemis carried off Iphigenia to serve as priestess of her temple, substituting a hind for the sacrifice. This episode from the Troy legend was dramatized by Euripides in his tragedy, *Iphigenia at Aulis*.

Another unfortunate incident in the Greek expedition against Troy was their inhuman abandoning of Philoctetes on the island of Lemnos because a snake bite had developed into a nauseating sore. (We have in the *Philoctetes* of Sophocles a stirring dramatization of the pathetic lot of Philoctetes on the deserted island.) A later day brought the Greeks dire need of their deserted comrade; he was the possessor of the bow with which Heracles had slain the Trojan monster. With the arrival of the expedition, Protesilaus, the first Greek to set foot on Trojan soil, met instant death at the hands of Hector and was soon followed in death by his faithful wife, Laodamia.

For ten years Troy and neighboring citadels in the Troad lay under siege and were subjected to attack. The *Iliad* recounts the siege of Troy during fifty-one days of the tenth year of the war, and closes *in mediis rebus* with the slaying of Hector by Achilles.

## PROSECUTION OF WAR

With Hector, gallant defender of the Trojan homeland, removed from the fray, Trojans and Greeks (while the unseen hand of Death hovered over their respective plans) marshalled new forces and devised new strategy.

Penthesilea led from Thrace in support of the Trojans a

6

band of her countrywomen, the Amazons; but she fell before Achilles. Her beauty in death moved Achilles, and when Thersites mocked him for being moved, Achilles struck Thersites dead. The next Trojan ally to fall before Achilles was Memnon, the son of Eos, goddess of the Dawn. At last Achilles himself, though vulnerable only in the heel, was slain by Paris. When Achilles' celebrated armor was awarded to Odysseus, Ajax, mentally unbalanced with disappointment, committed suicide. This episode in the story was made famous by the *Ajax* of Sophocles.

Now the Trojan, Helenus, the son of Priam, being endowed with prophetic powers, when captured in an ambush by Odysseus revealed that Troy could fall only when Philoctetes and Neoptolemus (the son of Achilles who was also called Pyrrhus) joined the Greeks. So the Greek Philoctetes was brought from his abandonment on Lemnos, and when he had been healed by Machaon, with the bow and arrows of Heracles he wounded Paris. The wife of Paris, Oenone, abandoned by him in favor of Helen, alone had the power to heal Paris, but refused to do so, though she later joined him in death. The young Neoptolemus, too, was brought from Scyros to Troy, and he drove the Trojans back within their walls.

The next objective of the Greeks was to get possession of the Palladium, a statue of Pallas Athena which had been in the city for several generations and was the gift of either Zeus or Athena. Its presence in the city insured the city's immunity to attack. The Greeks had been advised by Helenus to seize the Palladium. Helenus was angry at the Trojans because he was not given the hand of Helen after the death of Paris. Odysseus craftily entered Troy in the guise of a beggar and managed to spirit the Palladium out of the city. Helen recognized him in the prosecution of his mission but did not betray him to the Trojans.

The fall of Troy, for which the stage was now set, was effected by means of a hollow wooden horse suggested by Athena and built by Epeus. With its burden of Greek warriors inside, it was left on the plain outside the city as a supposed supplication to Athena for a safe return home. Instead of going home, the Greeks repaired to the near-by island of Tenedos to await a prearranged signal from Sinon. Trojan counsel regarding the disposition of the horse was divided, but when Laocoön, priest of Poseidon, proposed the destruction of it and actually struck it, the attack upon him by sea monsters was construed as a portent of divine displeasure; and so the horse was jubilantly brought into the citadel. When the horse was inside the city, the Greek forces within and without the city joined; universal pillage and massacre followed.

The return of the Greek heroes to their homes has provided, too, a broad field of legend for artists, just as did the story of the Trojan War. The most famous of the poems on this subject still is the *Odyssey* of Homer.

# II. THE LEGEND IN HOMER AND IN THE CYCLIC EPICS

THE *Iliad* begins with the wrath of Achilles, son of Peleus, over the impending forfeiture to Agamemnon of the captive maiden, Briseis, and Achilles' consequent withdrawal from the fray. The slaying of Patroclus clad in the armor of Achilles induces Achilles to return to the field of battle, and leads eventually to the slaying of Hector, the ransoming of Hector's corpse by his aged father Priam, and the burial of Hector. With the burial the *Iliad* closes. In the *Odyssey* Troy serves passively as a *terminus post quem*. After having spent ten years with the Greek forces at Troy the crafty Odysseus was forced by Poseidon to wander over the high seas for another decade, constantly delayed in his effort to return to his home and family. The action of the *Odyssey* occupies only about six weeks in the tenth year of its hero's wanderings, although the classic tale recounted by Odysseus at the palace of King Alcinoüs carries one back to his departure from Troy. At its close the *Odyssey* leaves Odysseus avenged on the suitors who had beset and possessed his ancestral estate.

## Epic Tradition and Importance of Homer

The exhaustive excavations carried out at Troy under the direction of Schliemann, Dörpfeld, and Blegen have established beyond doubt the historical reality of Troy. That the *Iliad* has some core of historical fact may be accepted with assurance, although fortunately that core is not our problem.

Nor can there be any reasonable doubt that Homer stands at the end of a long epic and poetic development both in the Motherland and in Ionia. The songs of traveling Achaean minstrels, who preceded Homer, must be regarded as a link, now irretrievably lost, connecting Homer with the heroic age of the thirteenth and twelfth centuries B.C., of which he sings.

While the content of the *Iliad* and *Odyssey* is traditional and basically historical, the greatness of these poems is established in another court than that of literal historical truth. Schliemann need not have run around the citadel of Troy, at least to establish the validity of Homer's story or his theory regarding its site. If he ran for the exercise, he should not be begrudged that. Basically it is not Troy which sheds glory upon Homer, but Homer and the epic tradition upon Troy. The discovery of Troy and the discoveries at Troy have their own importance, but the greatness of Homer's poems and of their tradition was established long before.

Before venturing into the far-flung ramifications of the legend of Troy in the various arts, however, it seems in place here, as a result of the new interest in the Homeric poems which the recent excavations at Troy have aroused, to comprehend broadly the startling significance of the *Iliad* and *Odyssey* in the realm of the esthetic and the human. What purposes these stories serve or what form they take in later times remains to be seen, but a glance at Byron's flippant lines on the *Odyssey*[1] brings one back to Homer with gratitude.

POETRY.—As a poet Homer belongs not to poets alone, but to the world at large. It is still refreshing to come back to Homer from the things written about him. Here were a poet and a poetic tradition centuries before we have a recorded use of the Greek word for poet. Nor was there any great body of literary theory about poetry until those distant times nearer our own when men no longer able to be poets were better qualified to classify and analyze both poets and their poems.

Poetic genius in the Homeric poems manifests itself both in the small and in the large. The verse is varied, convincing, and melodious, and in its tempo it bears some relation to the dominant mood and thought of what the poet sings. It can be heavy or light, fast or slow, both in a line or passage. Through his similes and epithets the poet has added artistry to his narrative. Upon nature and the trades he draws for both poetic and dramatic effects. Both he sees with the imaginative eye of the poet and not with the calculating eye of a materialist. It remained for a modern poet to say that there are starry uses of stars, but Homer knew how to transmute the stars into poetry and to ennoble his heroes in comparison with them. The Homeric rosy-fingered Dawn, white-armed Hera, golden-throned Artemis, and silver-footed Thetis have since the days of Chapman found worthy successors in Gray's incense-breathing morn, Shelley's rainbow-skirted shower, Keats' azure-lidded sleep, and Emerson's bud-crowned spring. A shadow may have asked its fellow shadow whether it believed in people, but a poet who wants to sing of the silver-footed Thetis who dwells in the wide bosom of the sea attended by her bevy of nymphs, or of the archer-goddess Artemis who moves over the ridges of Taÿgetus or over long Erymanthus in the company of the nymph-daughters of aegis-bearing Zeus may not falter as he moves into the higher reality of imaginative fiction. Sound has a chance in Homer, being associated with melody and rhythm; motion, being related to purpose; beauty, being united with truth and values. In this kind of poetic creativeness both man and life cease to be disastrous in their implications and justify one's faith in human destiny. The striking beauty of the Aegean as travelers to Greece know it must compete with the poet's conception of his native sea as he describes it early in the eighteenth book of the *Iliad*. Homer would have understood and enjoyed the lines of Byron:

> The beings of the mind are not of clay;
> Essentially immortal, they create
> And multiply in us a brighter ray
> And more beloved existence.[2]

In their sustained inspiration, their unfaltering faith in the reality of the unseen, and their capacity to reproduce the shocking horrors of war and the prosaic manifestations of nature and of human life and to re-create them as poetry, the Homeric poems stand out magnificently, seldom equaled and never surpassed, in the long tradition of which they are for us the beginning. Their poetry is not tinsel; it comes out of an authentic tradition of poetic creativeness. The importance of the Homeric poems, then, is not *what* they relate, but *how* they relate it.

HUMANITY.—In addition to being inspired poems of the first magnitude, the Homeric poems are pre-eminently human documents. Their humanity has helped to keep man humane during the ages. Other ages in re-dressing the Homeric poems according to contemporary *mores* have been only partially successful in preserving either their poetry or their humanity. In general, the Greek artist was born with a high capacity for disengaged reflection about man; this trait is evident in the Homeric poems. Naturally, there is wealth in these poems, and there are good and bad uses of it; there are men who hate one another like black death for good and bad reasons; there are women of different social positions for reasons not always of their own choosing; and there is marriage, which has seldom been a chapter in the emancipation of women. Homer does not ignore distinctions between men and women in their different environments of wealth, social position, sex, and race, but he does transcend them. His men and women are in their supreme moments men and women, not footnotes to wealth or symbols of a social class, sex, or race. It might be admitted in passing that the history of woman in either European life or literature, ancient or modern, is not particularly encouraging. It has been a man's world. Where does one go to find a set of women to match Homer's immortal creations, whether for their mature social poise, responsibility, good taste, emotional sensitiveness, or for the lack of the many qualities which leave the women of many periods of literature as dated anachronisms in later times? Homer's men and women have no philosophical background to help them see a common element of humanity in one another; they discover this in their own empirical way and provide a convincing picture of humanity for later philosophers. Two examples of this trait of the Homeric poems may be cited.

All readers remember the sublimating humanity of those two jewels of the *Iliad,* the parting scene of Hector from his wife and child and the meeting of the aged, heartbroken Priam with Achilles in Achilles' tent. In the first of these scenes Hector, dressed in a bronze helmet with a nodding horsehair crest, ceases in the eyes of the baby Astyanax to be his father, and the child shrinks back to the bosom of his nurse in dread until his father removes the helmet; nor does the plumage of war exempt Andromache and Hector from a keen sense of their poignant sadness—the price of being human—as they anticipate the fickleness and caprice of war. Both know that

> Between two worlds life hovers like a star,
> 'Twixt night and morn, upon the horizon's verge

and they are drawn together both by their own need for comfort in the face of the bleakness of destiny and by the desire to protect their baby, whose helplessness and unawareness increases their own pathos and their own sense of responsibility for him and for each other.

Through his moving story of the ransoming of the dead Hector by Priam at the close of the *Iliad* Homer similarly conveys to the Greek world a simple but profound and unforgettable message of man's need of humility and compassion. Both Herodotus and Sophocles in later days re-echo this Homeric lesson. Bitter enemies though they were, Priam and Achilles find common ground of friendship in their awareness of the afflictions which a malignant destiny sets upon them. As Priam falls weeping at the feet of Achilles, Achilles also weeps, and with pity and counsel raises the aged man from the ground. Achilles has his handmaidens bathe the corpse, and then he himself covers it and lays it on the polished wagon of Priam. In the touching humanity of this sublime scene the trappings of royalty and the pride of victory can be only irrelevant intrusions. The unique thing about the Homeric poems is that out of the degradation of war and its intense hatred a scene of spiritual beauty flowers.

ROUNDED CHARACTER CREATIONS.—Homer not only attains humanity in his characters, but he makes them happily balanced people. Achilles is an extraordinary synthesis of contradictory qualities. For his physical prowess Greek and Trojan alike have equal respect. His shout, clear as the sound of a clarion, struck terror into the hearts of the Trojans even in the flush of victory. As a man of independent judgment, he will not be bullied by an overbearing superior. An effront to his personal rights throws him into wrath which only the death of his dearest friend dissolves. His fortitude and courage in facing adversaries, human and divine, are drawn in generous epic proportions. He even looks death in the eye without quailing. But at the same time there is a softer and warmer side to Achilles. Heralds found him playing his lyre—as sure a mark of a gentleman in that day as the wearing of lace in another day. In the presence of his goddess mother he is like a child, and tears come to him easily as an expression of his desire for solace and protection in a disturbing world. Homer's reticence in this and other matters need not obscure for us the feeling of the captive Briseis for Achilles, even though the poet expresses this feeling in a single word. She was as "unwilling" to leave Achilles as he was to let her go. Even Agamemnon's heralds, Talthybius and Eurybates, go to fetch Briseis unwillingly and stand in the presence of Achilles with dread and reverence. The devotion of them all to Achilles in contrast with their silence regarding Agamemnon represents a triumph of the spirit, a triumph of nobility, even in defeat, over ignobility, even in success.

Another blending agent in the characterization of Achilles is his destiny to die early in life as a consequence of his victory over Hector. His was a pathetic sadness which found the sting of mortality even in divine lineage and of defeat even in victory. And yet despair and sadness are only fleeting shadows in Homer's portrayal of Achilles; of frustration and cynicism Achilles knows nothing. The emotions of Achilles are simple but profound, not complex or subtle. He bears the strains upon them as does a rubber band which is subjected to strain for the first, not the last time. While deep emotions arise in the Homeric poems, they find expression easily.

In Homer's Achilles, then, we find physical might and hard mental qualities accompanied and relieved by emotional softness and warmth. And regardless of whether there once was a real Achilles, Homer's Achilles has come to us out of a poetic tradition, and is an honor to it.

DRAMATIC POWER.—Another of the sterling qualities of Homer is his dramatic power. His story is one of men impelled by deep emotions and steady wills, but in the true epic tradition it is also a broad chapter in the history of Providence. Men play the game. The action is intense because men's spirits are magnificently undaunted in the face of superhuman work, extreme sacrifice, and mortal danger. Momentous crises of physical action, constructed along broad epic lines, involve the active participation of gods and Fate. The gods act in various capacities as coaches, substitutes, umpires, spectators, and spongers. Their direct intervention, aside from the artistic effect, broadens the scope and intensifies the sweep of the action. Fate marks off the gridiron. Its presence, however remote, lends purpose and goal to the story without detracting from its vitality; for vital decisions and initiative rest in the hands of men. The simile augments the strenuousness of the action at every turn by constant translation of action in terms of natural forces within the knowledge and sometimes beyond the capacities of men. Rhetoric, that pale and artificial substitute for "the sweat, blood, and tears" of real action, is as yet undeveloped; and social awareness has not yet undermined the poet's zest for war as a literary subject.

Natural Realism.—Sublime though they be, the Homeric poems are realistic. In the portrayal of nature and animals Homer shows himself a close observer. Students of Greece know that he is genuine and that he rings true to his land. He is not a poet of lace and ruffles and he does not ignore the commonplace; indeed, he uses the world about him for marked dramatic and artistic effects. That everyday things are dull is a discovery of the ignoble and not of the creative mind. Through his similes Homer portrays with graphic vividness in the heat of their respective activities swarming bees, geese, cranes, and long-necked swans, flies buzzing around pails of new milk in the springtime, flocks in the pastures, bull, steed, lion, serpent, boar, hawk, oxen, wolves, wasps, and hounds. Upon nature he draws for the west wind in the cornfield, the

East wall of Troy VI. Courtesy of Dr. Carl W. Blegen. See page 9

*Tabula Iliaca.* Capitoline Museum, Rome. See page 27

waves of the sea, the forest fire on a mountaintop, mist, cloud, wintry torrents, snowflakes, the falling oak tree, and the heaven studded with stars around the shining moon. Ajax, son of Telamon, in the battle for possession of the Greek ships is compared in rapid succession with a wild beast giving way step by step, with a tawny lion departing frustrated at dawn from a herd guarded against him, and with a lazy ass disregarding the blows of the boys attending him. References to the simple crafts, trades, and occupations of the countryside also show Homer to be a close observer and true portrayer of such activities. He is capable of realism in small detail; and yet this realism does not mar, but makes authentic the beauty, the truth, and the idealism of his narrative as a whole.

A fair measure of Homer's use of commonplace, even shabby things, may be seen in his portrayal of Argus, Odysseus' dog. It should be said in passing that few things are more degraded and ill-tempered in the European tradition than the dog, and the tradition of the Greek dog is hardly that of our parlor showpiece. When Odysseus returned to his palace after his long absence of twenty years, his old friend Argus, whom he had left as a puppy, alone recognized him. The dog, full of fleas, lay upon a dung-pile. (In Pope it seems to be a rich manure which is "obscene with reptiles.") When his master approached conversing with his faithful swineherd Eumaeus, Argus raised his head and ears and wagged his tail, but was too weak to move toward his master. Fearful of revealing his identity even to Eumaeus, Odysseus was unable to greet his dog, and turning aside he furtively wiped away a tear as he entered his palace. Argus' soul passed to the halls of dark death, failing to survive the emotion of seeing his master.

IDEALISM.—Homer has portrayed his people with remarkable fidelity, too. It is the work of a camera to reproduce life with unrelieved literalness, but of a great poet to lift life above

17

the petty annoyances which dull its outline and mar its beauty. Had Homer done less, he would not have been true either to his own people or to the highest capacities of human life, which he helps us to understand. This ability of Homer's we may call a sustained and faithful idealism. Men and women can still be ugly in Homer, and unscrupulous, short-tempered, domineering, unfaithful, bigoted, and craven; but they also succeed in becoming noble, self-sacrificing, loving, well-bred, humble, reflective, faithful to a trust, and dignified. Their beauty and poise are not external but instinctive; their courage does not flinch before defeat or death; their resolution and initiative are undaunted by the opposition of the very gods. Their nobility adheres to no strict demarcation of social class; their gentility is not limited to men or to women; and their sense of fair play does not exclude the enemy or the foreigner. For Homer clothes and wealth are not satisfactory substitutes for humanity, nor race and sex complete criteria in the determining of humanity. Despite the shadows and fears which lower over him, Homeric man is confident of the efficacy of his wit, cunning, and intelligence in meeting the obstacles which confront him. In giving us his Achilles, Hector, Helen, Priam, Odysseus, Nausicaa, Eumaeus, Penelope, and Eurycleia, Homer, at the dawn of Western culture, has contributed in some measure to the making of a master yardstick against which the humanity of man can be measured.

SUMMARY OF HOMERIC QUALITIES.—In conclusion, the Homeric poems represent fairly the early age out of which they come. They emphasize outer action and simplify the inner psychological motivations and the moral code. For morality in Homer has to do directly with man's relation to his fellow man. The gods are not symbols or agents of it. Among the cardinal virtues of the Homeric man are hospitality, bravery, wisdom, love of home and family, and personal honor. Particularly reprehensible in the Homeric code are disregard of a sworn oath; failure to accord due respect to mother, father, stranger, and suppliant; and arrogant pride. The end of morality in Homer is not the winning of divine favor, but the preservation of human life and civilization universally on a rational and social basis.[3]

The Homeric poems are brilliantly prophetic of the coming greatness of Greek literature in their capacity to transmute the prose of living into the poetry of imaginative experience, in the lucidity with which they visualize the divine apart from mysticism and degrading fear, and in their wholesome catholicity at seeing humanity in man irrespective of his race, sex, or social position. At no later time is the story of Troy endowed so richly with the qualities of poetic imagination, dramatic conviction, and essential humanity.[4] To their race the Homeric poems bequeathed the wisdom of distilled experience. They taught their people an awareness of the strength of humility, of the sadness of human destiny because of both the limitations and the realizable goals of living, and of the beauty of the commonplace. In these many respects Homer is the father of the Hellenic spirit.

## FALL OF TROY IN HOMER

While Homer is not concerned directly with the fall of Troy, inasmuch as the *Iliad* closes before that event and the *Odyssey* opens after it, yet he does reveal a familiarity with many details of the last days of the city. It seems pertinent to append at this point such facts as Homer supplies on the subject. Aeneas is listed in the catalogue of ships in the early part of the *Iliad* as the leader of the Dardanians and as accompanied by the two sons of Antenor.[5] He is said to bear a perpetual hatred for Priam because Priam paid him no honor at all, in spite of all his valor among men.[6] Achilles taunts Aeneas as cherishing a hope of some day coming into Priam's sovereignty over the Trojans,[7] and a striking passage in the same episode singles out Aeneas to survive the Trojan War and to hand down to his children's children his sovereign sway over the Trojans. In this passage, with Aeneas hard pressed by Achilles, Poseidon goes to the immortal gods with an appeal to rescue Aeneas because of the destiny marked out for him.[8] Antenor, too, seems destined for consideration from the Greeks because of the hospitality which he had once extended to Odysseus and Menelaus on the occasion of their official mission to Troy.[9] That his soul is not in the war is also evident from his counsel to the Trojans to return Helen and her wealth to the sons of Atreus.[10] When Telemachus went to the palace of Menelaus at Sparta to inquire concerning his father, Odysseus, Helen told him of the daring visit of Odysseus within the walls of Troy in the guise of a beggar, and how she recognized but did not betray him;[11] and Menelaus recalled to his young guest the shrewdness of Odysseus in restraining his comrades in silence while Helen, standing by the wooden horse, called to the warriors within, feigning the voices of their wives.[12] The bard Demodocus at the court of Alcinoüs in answer to the request of Odysseus sang of the fall of Troy, beginning with the wooden horse.[13] Meeting the shade of Achilles in the lower world Odysseus consoled his departed friend with a commendation of the courage of his son Neoptolemus while in the wooden horse, contrasting this courage with the craven fear shown by his comrades, and he assured Achilles of his son's survival of the Trojan campaign.[14] Characteristic of the simplicity of the Homeric poems is their interest in the wooden horse as a stratagem apart from any marked religious significance. Neither Sinon nor Laocoön is mentioned in the Homeric poems, but then, as was stated above, the fall of Troy does not come within the province of either poem.

# HOMER AND THE CYCLIC EPICS

## The Cyclic Epics

The *Iliad* and the *Odyssey* served for later bards as nuclei around which other epics gathered out of the wealth of legends which the early Greeks inherited from their heroic past. The deeds and heroes left unsung in the *Iliad* and the *Odyssey* supplied the stuff for the bards of the epic cycle, as these lost poems are collectively called. What they lacked in inspiration they undoubtedly compensated for amply by scholarly inclusiveness and epic correctness, and regardless of their lack of poetic or artistic merit they became an important mine of source material for later use in the arts. Although these later epics have disappeared save for the barest of fragments, they became to antiquity a part of the Homeric tradition and they greatly enriched the scope of the Trojan legend.

Throughout the entire course of the ancient Greek and Roman world no fine line of distinction can be drawn between Homer and the cyclic poets. Those epics in which was unfolded the story of the Trojan War from the plan of Zeus for a purge of an overpopulated world to the return of the Greek heroes to their homes at the end of the war are among these works of the cyclic poets.

*Cypria.*—Herodotus was the first to question the Homeric authorship of the *Cypria*. The *Cypria* related many of the episodes in the Trojan legend down to the point where the *Iliad* began, including the plan of Zeus to relieve overpopulation by starting a war, the presence of Eris at the wedding of Peleus and Thetis, the beauty contest of the three goddesses, the judgment of Paris and the award made by him to Aphrodite, the seduction and abduction of Helen, the mustering of the Greek forces at Aulis, the attempted sacrifice of Iphigenia and her rescue by Artemis, the abandonment of Philoctetes on Lemnos, the deaths of Protesilaus and Troilus, and Zeus' plan to help the Trojans by effecting the withdrawal of Achilles. Telephus and Palamedes also played rôles in the *Cypria*, which provides an introduction to the *Iliad*.

*Aethiopis.*—The *Aethiopis*, written by Arctinus, dovetailed perfectly into the end of the *Iliad*. It opened with the coming of Penthesilea to aid Priam and her slaying by Achilles. When taunted by Thersites for being moved by the beauty of the fallen queen Achilles slew him. Memnon of Aethiopia next arrived to aid the Trojans, and was also slain by Achilles. Achilles met his untimely end at the hands of Paris and Apollo. He received due burial, but in the course of the rites Odysseus and Ajax both claimed their comrade's armor.

*Little Iliad* and *Sack of Ilium.*—The *Little Iliad*, attributed to Lesches, opened with the subject of Sophocles' *Ajax*, the award of Achilles' armor to Odysseus, and the consequent suicide of Ajax. As a result of a prophecy of the captured Helenus, Philoctetes was brought from Lemnos to Troy, where he slew Paris. Helen then married Deiphobus, and Neoptolemus was brought to Troy to deal the final telling blow. The legend of Troy's fall from this point was elaborated in considerable detail in both this poem and in Arctinus' *Sack of Ilium*, which was a continuation of his *Aethiopis*.[15] In the *Sack of Ilium* Odysseus entered Troy as a beggar and while inside had the active co-operation of Helen. The theft of the Palladium by Diomedes and Odysseus followed this mission. Then the Greeks sailed away temporarily to Tenedos, leaving the wooden horse behind. A scene on the Trojan Tablet, a marble relief ascribed to the first century A.D., which professes to derive from the *Little Iliad* shows the horse being brought into Troy in a way reminiscent of the corresponding scene of festal joy in the *Aeneid*.[16] Trojans and Phrygians draw the horse into the city with a rope as Priam leads the way and attendant women dance. Sinon standing close by apparently is having his bonds untied. Cassandra at the Scaean gate gesticulates wildly in futile warning. While both the Sinon and Laocoön episodes belonged to the legend in these early days, the stirring dramatic, psychological, and rhetorical possibilities inherent in them seem, quite naturally, to have been left unexploited. Since the Trojans took the horse into their city before determining what disposition to make of it, Sinon, who had been taken prisoner while the Trojans were bearing it within the walls, had to be saved for the later rôle of signaling to the Greeks at Tenedos. In the *Sack of Ilium* two snakes killed Laocoön and one of his sons, but only after the horse had been admitted. Presaging in the fate of Laocoön, an evil omen, Aeneas fled to Mt. Ida with his followers. Then followed the signal of Sinon by torchlight to the Greeks at Tenedos,[17] the joining of Greek forces inside and outside the city, and the sacking of the city under bright moonlight.

According to Arctinus and Stesichorus, and the usual tradition coming from them, amid the destruction of Troy Priam fell at the hands of Neoptolemus at the altar of Zeus; but according to Lesches he fell at the door of his palace. Having slain Deiphobus, Menelaus led Helen to the ships. In the narrative of Demodocus in the *Odyssey*, too, Menelaus and Odysseus set out for the palace of Deiphobus to slay him.[18] Ajax, son of Oïleus, carried off Cassandra from the shrine of Athena, and in so doing overturned the statue of the goddess to which Cassandra was clinging and thereby incurred the anger even of his fellow-Greeks. As Homer knew,[19] the wrath of Athena and Poseidon was to attend Ajax on his return home; and readers of Vergil will remember Juno's angry reference to the fate of Ajax at the hands of Athena.[20] Polyxena, the daughter of Priam and Hecuba, was sacrificed at the tomb of Achilles, and Astyanax, the young son of Hector and Andromache, also was killed. In the *Sack of Ilium* Odysseus killed Astyanax, but in the *Little Iliad* Neoptolemus snatched him from his mother's lap and threw him by the ankle from the wall. Into the hands of Neoptolemus fell Andromache and Aeneas. In the poem of Lesches, Lycaon, the son of Antenor, wounded during the confusion, was recognized by Odysseus and carried to safety. After Neoptolemus was slain at Delphi by Orestes, Aeneas, set free, lived in Macedonia. In the *Little Iliad* Aeneas' wife was named Eurydice.

It is quite impossible to reconstruct a continuous story out of such sporadic fragments, which have, moreover, come down to us with rather flimsy documentation; but it is clear that early Greece had a complete account—and, in part, conflicting accounts—of the fall of Troy. That there would be more interest in outer action than in nice relationships of cause and effect we might take for granted. The artists who used the material of these poems in later times wanted the story, primarily. Lack of poetic or artistic merit in the source need not necessarily have disturbed them. Whatever they wanted to add of their own in the way of spirit and interpretation, they were free, therefore, to add. It will be observed that in the epic cycle Aeneas is a person apart. In good season he fled from the catastrophe and worked out his future in Macedonia.

*Returns* and *Telegonia.*—The *Returns* related the fortunes of Menelaus, Agamemnon, the Locrian Ajax, Neoptolemus, and others during and upon their return home. The *Telegonia* derives its name from Telegonus, the son of Odysseus and Circe, who wandering in search of his father, unwittingly slew him during an attack upon Ithaca. Its author was Eugammon of Cyrene, who lived at the end of the seventh century B.C.

# III. THE LEGEND IN LITERATURE

M AN has been eager always to see himself, especially if in so doing he may be spared the literal chemistry of what he is and may see himself as he would like to be. He who goes to a poor mirror will see only the mirror, which thereby fails to serve its purpose; but he who goes to a good mirror will see himself, as he expected, and if all is well, he will come away reassured. The Greek epic tradition regarding Troy has been the best of mirrors. The many-sided genius of Homer, its central unit, has never been exhausted. Proof of its worth rests in its unique capacity out of the infinity of its lights and shadows to honor with a faithful reproduction the many different types of human life and activity which have come to it to see and have gone away satisfied, reassured, and inspired. Seldom has it been the purpose of writers simply to understand and reproduce Homer, though an academic interest in him or even in some small phase of his work has never had to apologize for itself. Indeed, few ages have had the mental and spiritual equipment to comprehend Homer fully. Seldom have the contributions of writers to the Homeric story been as great as the original qualities which Homer molded into his story. Seldom would it be desirable for these writers to set themselves up as mirrors to replace Homer, for they could only distort other ages or represent them partially. The tradition of Homer in general has not been an academic study of a dead past, but a tradition of implementing the skills and energizing the perceptions of the present through the past. For example, the Russian novelist of the early nineteenth century, Gogol, would not have written *Taras Bulba* without the inspiration of the *Odyssey*. The unveiling of the *Odyssey* to Russia at this time gave this formless land with all its grotesque bigness, pettiness, and injustice a chance to see and correct itself in the light of form, heroic stature, and poetic justice. The non-Homeric parts of the Greek epic tradition regarding Troy acquired some of their reflecting qualities through their proximity to Homer. But within themselves the cyclic epics while they survived had the content which made them a satisfactory mirror of those commonly recurring human activities and interests of war, travel, pathos, and love. Some ages have been so far removed from the text and language of Homer that they could not distinguish him from the cyclic poets, who were themselves known only vaguely, if at all.

## Greek Lyric Poetry

In the hearts of the Greeks the melody of Homeric song lingered on through many ages. To them his character creations never lost their vivid reality. The Greek lyric poets from Asia Minor to Sicily and from the seventh to the fourth centuries B.C., preoccupied though they were with more immediate personal and civic problems, found the story of Troy constantly haunting their imaginations.

Stesichorus.—Stesichorus, whose life in Sicily bridged the seventh and sixth centuries B.C., won conspicuous renown in the Greek tradition for making his lyre bear the burden of epic song. Quintilian in a famous dictum speaks of Stesichorus as *maxima bella et clarissimos canentem duces et epici carminis onera lyrā sustinentem.*[1] A slanderous poem of Stesichorus on Helen, according to legend, brought blindness to the poet as punishment; but when the bard retracted his scurrilous remarks to the point of stating that Helen never even went to Troy, his sight was restored immediately.[2]

Stesichorus also wrote a poem on the sack of Troy, a few details of which survive in references by various Greek writers and on the Trojan Tablet. This tablet, known as the *tabula Iliaca,* in the Capitoline Museum at Rome is assigned to the first century A.D. It was found at Bovillae on the Appian Way in the seventeenth century, and contains reliefs illustrating the sack of Troy according to the authority of both the *Little Iliad* and of Stesichorus, as is stated on the tablet itself. The city of Troy is depicted with walls, battlements, a gate, houses, a temple of Athena girt with a colonnade, and the court of Priam's palace with a colonnade flanked on one side by a shrine of Aphrodite and on the other by an unspecified shrine. In the precinct of the temple of Athena the Greeks, descending from the wooden horse by means of a ladder, enter the fray. Ajax, son of Oïleus, drags Cassandra by the hair from the steps of the temple as she stretches out her arms in appeal to the goddess. Other Greeks are coming into the precinct from the outside. Priam is being slain by Neoptolemus at the altar in the court of his palace. Hecuba at his side is being dragged away by a Greek soldier. Outside the colonnade Helen is seized by Menelaus as she sought refuge at the shrine of Aphrodite. In a lower scene Aeneas escapes with his household gods stored in a chest. At the bottom of the relief in the center is the Scaean gate. With Hermes leading the way Aeneas follows. On his shoulders he has Anchises, who holds the household gods. Aeneas leads Ascanius by the hand, and Creusa, weeping, follows behind. Outside the walls are two tombs, that of Achilles on the right and that of Hector on the left. At the tomb of Hector are assembled Talthybius, Andromache, Cassandra, and Helenus. On the side of the tomb we see that Odysseus has arrived to announce in the presence of Helenus, Andromache, Hecuba, and Polyxena that the latter must be sacrificed. At the tomb of Achilles Neoptolemus slays Polyxena, while Odysseus, head in hand, sits, and Calchas stands near by. In the right-hand corner below the tomb is represented the departure of Aeneas at the headland of Sigeum. Anchises carries into the boat (which is well stocked with provisions) the chests containing the sacred images. Aeneas follows up the gangplank holding Ascanius by the hand. The pilot Misenus comes along behind with a steering paddle. The inscription above the head of Misenus states that Aeneas is sailing to Hesperia.

Professor Bowra in his recent study of Greek lyric poetry[3] assigns to this tablet a post-Vergilian date rather than the pre-Vergilian date customarily assigned to it. If the tablet is post-Vergilian, it is difficult to feel that it could have been made without having been influenced by Vergil's narrative, both as a general proposition and especially in view of the close identity of the two versions; and it is also easy to share Professor Bowra's hesitancy about attributing such an elaborate and exact anticipation of Vergil to Stesichorus at such an early time. No definite solution of the reliability of the tablet is possible with so much of Vergil's source material irretrievably lost, but one should not argue too strongly from the absence in extant pre-Vergilian Greek poetry of references to the departure of Aeneas from Troy. Both Greek and Etruscan vases and gems and Greek coins survive which show the departure of Aeneas to have been a popular theme for portrayal.[4]

SAPPHO, ALCAEUS.—The inimitable lyric poetess Sappho, a native of the island of Lesbos around the turn of the seventh century B.C., re-created some of our legend's characters in terms of her own subjective, erotic interests. In one of her more recently found fragments she sings that while to some the fairest thing on the dark earth is a host of cavalry or infantry or a fleet of ships, to her it is one's lover. By the reckless love of Helen for Paris she illustrates her point.[5] The prayer of the Greek chieftains to Hera after their destruction of Troy, without which they would have been unable to return home, is clearly the content of another fragment of Sappho.[6] Still another fragment attributed to Sappho, a lovely one of considerable length rescued from a third century papyrus, describes in exquisite detail the arrival of Hector at Troy accompanied by his new bride Andromache, and the enthusiastic welcoming of them into the city amid the gaiety and festal merriment appropriate to the occasion.[7] Among the more recently discovered fragments of Alcaeus, who was a compatriot and approximate contemporary of Sappho, is one which contrasts the joy which Thetis brought to the home of Peleus with the woe visited upon Troy by Helen.[8]

IBYCUS.—A sizable fragment of the middle of the sixth century B.C., by Ibycus, whose name is associated with Polycrates, the celebrated tyrant of Samos, pays tribute to the glory and eternal beauty of the legend of Troy and of those who participated in its siege, defense, and fall—a story to the telling of which only the Muses of Helicon could aspire. With deft skill he passes over the names of the flaxen-haired Helen, Priam, Zeus, Aphrodite, Paris, the slim-ankled Cassandra, Agamemnon, Menelaus, Achilles, and Ajax, son of Telamon; and in conclusion promises to Polycrates through his song the same undying glory which Homer gave to the heroes of Troy.[9]

PINDAR, BACCHYLIDES.—Pindar, the self-styled eagle of the lyric bards of Greece, on several occasions finds in the glorification of the ancestral heroes of Greece an opportunity to retrace the familiar outlines of the Trojan story from the building of the walls of Troy to its destruction and the scattering of its inhabitants.[10]

One of the dithyrambs of Bacchylides, the younger rival of

Pindar, deals with the embassy of Odysseus and Menelaus to Troy from the seat of the Greek camp at Tenedos for the purpose of demanding the return of Helen. Menelaus here reminds the Trojans that it is not high-ruling Zeus who is the cause of the great woes of mortal men, but unfearing recklessness.[11] Both Pindar and Bacchylides used the legend that the actual fall of Troy came through Philoctetes and his use of the bow of Heracles.[12] A few lines of Pindar's passage run:

"Thus do they say that god-like heroes went to bring from Lemnos the bowman son of Poeas, who was wearied with his wound, but who yet sacked the city of Priam, and ended the toil of the Danai, though he went on his way with a frame that was weak; but thus was it ordered of Fate."[13]

In one of his odes Bacchylides glorifies Aegina through its valiant heroes Peleus and Telamon and their sons, Achilles and Ajax. From this point the poet sketches in lovely lines the heroic stand of Ajax against the Trojans attacking the Greek fleet, and the reason for the withdrawal of Achilles from the fray. Illustrating the sense of relief felt by the Trojans in the absence of Achilles with a beautiful simile—more Homeric than anything else in Greek lyric poetry—of the joy which fills men's hearts when with the coming of dawn the north wind ceases to lash the sea and the south wind carries them to their unexpected haven, Bacchylides envisions the hopes of the Trojans in flush of victory—hopes soon to come to naught.[14]

## GREEK TRAGEDY

The Athenians in the fifth century added another memorable chapter to their spiritual history in the perfecting of tragedy. Since in origin tragedy had grown out of the dithyramb, the continuity of the lyric tradition was maintained. Using the epic legends as the material and the lyric tradition as a method of interpretation, Greek tragedy combined the two into a new form wherein epic heroes of old lived with the emotional intensity of their remote descendants in modern opera, in the unconscious fulfillment of destinies conceived for them by poet-philosophers. Thus the growing mind and the deepening soul of the Athenians invested in the Trojan story abundant expression of their conception of life as an artistic venture in the realm of the imaginative reason. From the simple objectivity of the epic to the intense subjectivity of the lyric and on to the projection of the individual into the conflicting passions inherent in his struggle against Fate or himself, the heroes and heroines of the Trojan War stepped out of the unfeeling oblivion of the past to serve as carriers in Greek tragedy for the highest of contemporary artistic and philosophic aspirations. Over one-fifth of the plays of Aeschylus and Euripides came from stories of the Trojan cycle, and Sophocles doubled this percentage.[15] Needless to say, a supreme experience for the Athenian tragic poets were the Homeric poems themselves.

AESCHYLUS.—Aeschylus is reputed to have acknowledged his indebtedness to Homer, although his real greatness, as that of Euripides, is independent of Homer and un-Homeric in nature. Of the Greek tragedians he is the prophet and moralist. Those who, like Pindar, Aeschylus, and Herodotus came through the ordeal of the Persian invasion carried in their hearts a devout faith in the works of Fate and the gods. The watchman in the memorable opening of the *Agamemnon* of Aeschylus catches sight from the roof of the palace at Argos of the beacon flares which announce the fall of Troy. Agamemnon and his captive maid Cassandra enter later, destined to witness more grievous woes than those they had suffered at Troy.

SOPHOCLES.—Sophocles was rightly regarded as the most

Homeric of the poets.[16] For his essential humanity, serenity, and restraint as a poet and philosopher he justly deserves that title. With Sophocles tragedy returned from the skies to the heart and mind of man. His characters, like those of Homer, exercise a forthright independence of action in their own name, and are not overshadowed by Fate as they are in Aeschylus or deflected from their central humanity as in Euripides. On the other hand, as would be expected, Sophoclean tragedy rises above Homer in its emphasis upon the human will as a battle-ground for the testing and occasionally for the purging of character. As Byron has said:

> And sterner hearts alone may feel
> The wound that time can never heal.
> The rugged metal of the mine
> Must burn before its surface shine.[17]

The *Philoctetes, Ajax,* and *Electra* of Sophocles are all a step removed from the actual fall of Troy, but some of his lost plays seem to have been concerned directly with that story, as, for example, the *Antenoridae, Laocoön, Polyxena, Priam,* and *Sinon.* Probably in the first of these lost plays the house of Antenor was marked by a leopard's skin as a symbol of immunity granted to Antenor himself and his family, who escaped to the Adriatic.[18] A fragment of the *Laocoön* refers to the escape of Aeneas with his father on his shoulders and attended by a large throng intent on the founding of a colony.[19] He had escaped just before the city was taken and made his way to Mt. Ida, having been warned by Anchises, who had reason to foresee the impending destruction of the city.[20]

EURIPIDES.—Euripides in his *Trojan Women* (415 B.C.) depicts the sufferings of the Trojan captives. The scene is laid on the shore of the Troad on the day following the fall of Troy. The play is virtually plotless, being a series of scenes

# THE LEGEND IN LITERATURE

Pierre Guérin. *Aeneas Relating to Dido the Disasters of Troy.*
Louvre, Paris. See page 38

> . . . he did discourse
> To love-sick Dido's sad attending ear
> The story of that baleful burning night
> When subtle Greeks surprised King Priam's Troy.

> —Shakespeare. *Titus Andronicus.* v. 3

Thetis and the Nereids bringing a shield, spear, and helmet to Achilles. Mosaic. Olynthus. Courtesy of Dr. David M. Robinson. See page 91

of grief and pathos relieved by Euripidean touches of realism, colloquialism, and sophistic logic in the spirit of Euripides himself, Voltaire, Shaw, and Erskine. The chorus, composed of captive women of Troy, sings a dramatic recital of the irony of the festive Trojans carrying into their city the wooden horse, an offering of pious homage to the very goddess who is working their undoing.[21] Cassandra, Polyxena, Hecuba, Astyanax, and Andromache all share in their city's ruin. Menelaus takes Helen back to Argos for punishment. Amid the wailing dirges of Hecuba and of the chorus as they are forced to the waiting ships the city behind them is fired and topples in ruins. The play is heavy with the feeling of the emptiness of victory even for the victors. Those who wish to re-create in their own minds the reaction of the original audience to this tragedy should do so in the light of its immediate historical background. The play was produced midway between the disgraceful Melian episode immortalized by Thucydides as a chapter in the spiritual degradation of Athens and the Sicilian expedition, which Thucydides again with the cold precision of a surgeon reveals as a manifestation of the overweening pride and ambition of Athens. There was a general weariness of war throughout the immediate period and an increasingly vocal yearning for some Utopia where humanity might find escape from its afflictions, as we know from several comedies of the period. The *Trojan Women* is said, however, to act well. Gilbert Murray, who is more than a critic of Euripides, finds a magnificent Aeschylean quality in the play.

Euripides' *Hecuba* also brings one into the shadow of Troy's fall. Detained on the coast of Thrace by adverse winds as they return home from Troy the Greeks are advised that the ghost of Achilles must be appeased with the sacrifice of a Trojan captive. The Greeks in council select Polyxena as the most fitting victim. One of the finest passages in Euripides is that in which Polyxena with sublime heroism bears her impending doom in the presence of the cynical and degenerate Odysseus. The second half of the play relates the discovery of the death of Polydorus, youngest son of Priam and Hecuba, who had been entrusted by his father along with considerable gold to the care of Polymestor, king of Thrace. Polymestor had betrayed the young boy, and Hecuba's horrible revenge on him follows. Vergil, too, makes Aeneas land in Thrace on his flight from Troy. The voice of Polydorus from the grave warned Aeneas to flee from that cruel land and greedy shore.[22]

In the *Andromache* of Euripides the sufferings attendant upon the destruction of Troy form a backdrop out of which Andromache comes to suffer further woes as the captive concubine of Neoptolemus in Thessaly. At the close of the tragedy Thetis appears to announce that Andromache, joined in wedlock with Helenus, must found in Epirus a new home and dynasty. Here in Vergil's version of the legend[23] Aeneas found Andromache and Helenus. Andromache lived on into the work of Racine and through him into the field of opera.

The *Helen* of Euripides reduces the Trojan War to utter futility. Its version is that already adumbrated in part by Hesiod, Stesichorus, and Herodotus:[24] that only a wraith of Helen went to Troy, and the real Helen spent the years of the war in Egypt, where Menelaus finally recovered her.

## HELLANICUS

A version of the fall of Troy was recorded by Hellanicus, a prominent chronicler of the fifth century B.C., in his account of the Trojan expedition. His interest in local traditions, together with his birth at Lesbos and residence on the mainland not far from Troy, lends peculiar significance to his version of the event as representing the tradition then current in the Troad. The heroic stature of Aeneas is evident in this

34

version now preserved in the *Roman Antiquities* of Dionysius of Halicarnassus, as follows:[25]

With the fall of the city the greater part of the Trojan and allied forces was slain in bed. Anticipating the impending tragedy Aeneas with his armed forces fled to the upper citadel called Pergamus while the Greeks were capturing the lower city. In the upper citadel were stored the holy objects of the Trojans and their wealth. This citadel served as a temporary refuge and as a gathering place for only temporary defense, and Aeneas while still there had time to evacuate women, children, the aged, and the infirm to Mt. Ida under the protection of a part of his army. In due time he retreated with the flower of his army, taking with him his father, the ancestral gods, his wife, and his children. The remnants of the Trojan forces assembled on Mt. Ida. The Greeks then made a truce with their foe stipulating that Aeneas and his followers should depart from the Troad in possession of whatever wealth they had saved from Troy. Aeneas accordingly embarked with his father and his sons (except for Ascanius) and sailed to Pallene. Dionysius regarded this version of the flight of Aeneas from Troy as the most trustworthy of them all, and informs us that it also is the one adopted by Hellanicus. In this account the entire responsibility for salvaging something out of the destruction of Troy fell upon Aeneas. His brilliance as a tactician brought him success in this, and his piety toward family and gods again reveals itself in his escape.

### Lycophron

In his obscure poem *Alexandra,* written in Greek in the form of a prophecy about 295 B.C., Lycophron makes Antenor a traitor to his country who will set a fire-signal and open the horse full of Greeks.[26] As we shall see later, this detail of the treachery of Antenor in betraying his country, the first ex-

ample occurring in extant literature, became an integral part
of the mediaeval versions of Troy's fall, where Aeneas was included as an accomplice of Antenor. In his account of the
tradition of Aeneas, Dionysius of Halicarnassus states that,
according to one Menecrates of Xanthus, Aeneas betrayed the
city of Troy to the Achaeans because of his hatred for Paris,
and that the grateful Achaeans allowed him to save his household. Aeneas, according to Menecrates, overthrew Priam because he had been rebuffed by Paris and cheated of his priv-
ileges, and then he became one of the Achaeans.[27] How considerable this tradition of the sabotage of Troy by Antenor
and Aeneas was we now have no way of telling. The entire
post-Vergilian tradition to this effect is thought to have pre-
Vergilian sources. Aeneas, according to Lycophron, will escape
from Troy and found Lavinium, which is his ultimate des-
tination. In attempting to carry off his household goods and
father to safety he is destined by his piety to provoke the admiration of the Greeks to the point that they will allow him
to choose and carry off whatever he wants.[28] According to
Varro in the first century B.C. Aeneas, granted *carte blanche*
to depart with whatever he wanted, first chose his father.
Admiring his piety the Greeks gave him another choice;
whereupon Aeneas selected the *penates*. This choice of his
so moved the Greeks that they then allowed him to go with
all his belongings.[29]

### EARLY ROMAN TRADITION

The reading and tradition of Homer and the Trojan legend
in general had never gone into eclipse during the interval of
four centuries which separates Greece and Rome at their best,
but the ebbing tide of decadent Greece and the rising tide of
Rome's fortunes carried with them no great poets of the first
rank save Theocritus. It will be necessary to pass over briefly

those minor Roman writers who from the early period of the Republic down into the Empire had been attracted to the Trojan legend as providing material for epic, tragedy, or merely translation, as, for example, Livius Andronicus, whose translation of the *Odyssey* long served as a text for schools, and Naevius, Ennius, Pacuvius, Accius, and Cn. Matius.[30] The Latin poet Naevius of the third century B.C. in some of the surviving fragments of his *Bellum Punicum* refers in retrospect to the departure from Troy of Aeneas, his wife, and his comrades.[31] In the last of the fragments referred to in note (31) King Latinus asks Aeneas how he had forsaken Troy. Ennius, too, in the beginning of his *Annals* passed in review the fall of Troy.[32] In early Roman tragedy, which leaned heavily on its Greek forerunner, the story of the fall of Troy enjoyed a considerable vogue. We know, by title at least, tragedies called the *Trojan Horse* by both Livius Andronicus, the father of Roman drama, and by Naevius; an *Andromache Prize of War* and a *Hecuba* by Ennius; and an *Antenoridae*, *Astyanax*, *Deiphobus*, and *Trojan Women* by Accius.

## VERGIL AND OVID

Vergil helps to transmit to the Middle Ages the epic and dramatic tradition of Greece. By his time the founding of Rome by the descendants of Aeneas had become political orthodoxy at Rome. Although by the time of Vergil whatever actual historical basis there may have been either for the destruction of Troy by the Greeks or the founding of Rome by the sons of Aeneas was hopelessly buried in oblivion, yet the weakness of the factual tradition was more than compensated by the fiction which had gathered around the historical conception. We are concerned here not with the historical truth of the legend, but simply with the legend itself. This story of the fall of Troy, evolved for and by the Greeks and accepted by the Romans long before the time of Vergil, was enshrined by Rome's greatest poet in Rome's greatest poem as historical background for the birth of Rome. Thus in the *Aeneid* the fall of Troy falls into a larger pattern of events in which Fate or Destiny spins the thread of a nation destined to flourish centuries after the time of Troy.

In the second book of the *Aeneid* Vergil places the narrative of Troy's fall on the lips of Aeneas, who relates it to Dido and her guests at dinner. Aeneas begins reluctantly and with sorrow still heavy on his soul. How he defended his city and family valiantly to the last and then lost all, and how he came to survive need not be repeated. Old though the story was, even in the time of Vergil, this new telling of it by the poet whom Shelley calls the dead king of melody, with its exacting workmanship, high idealism, majestic sadness, soulful music, and eloquent silences, is the most memorable chapter in its history. No staleness attended its appearance in the form which he gave it. On the contrary, stories told in the first person by important eyewitnesses have at least the outer structure of freshness. The chief successes of Vergil in his reworking of this legend are found in the new frame into which he sets the old picture, in his literary and philosophical interests, in the new organization of inner psychological forces and outer action for better dramatic effect, and in the new patriotism and national pride which come as a by-product of his story. Let us now take these points one by one:

The new frame put upon this picture of the fall of Troy—the romance of Aeneas and Dido—relieves with its new comfort and hope the unqualified tragedy and gloom of the traditional picture. The banquet at Dido's palace adds a ray of sunshine and the beauty of wistful melancholy to the darkened lives of Aeneas and Dido, and to Vergil's audience it adds a new spiritual depth in the "thoughts that do often lie too deep for human tears." At the same time the picture of the fall of Troy has been thrown into the background and merely serves as a reminder of the "blood and tears" out of which came the full glory of Rome, the real theme of the *Aeneid*. Both of these changes made by Vergil in the frame and in the picture of the fall of Troy relieve somewhat the dominant gloom and hopelessness of the traditional picture with a tragically sad touch of hope for Aeneas personally and with a feeling of pride felt by his Roman descendant. In Vergil the dying embers of one chapter in the annals of destiny—the fall of Troy—enkindle the love and hate of the first page of another chapter—the chapter of Aeneas and Dido. A generation which has seen the love of a king for a commoner rock an empire and startle the world should feel the poignancy of a situation in which the lovers are future founder and reigning queen of lands whose sons shall one day be mortal enemies.

While this new setting to a time-honored story lacked no sense of immediacy to the Roman reader, modern readers in many cases will interpret Aeneas' responsibility to Dido and to his mission in terms of contemporary ethics controlling such problems, and, naturally, the ethics of such a situation will change with the crossing of a national frontier or even of the railroad tracks. In all likelihood the romantic tradition of Hollywood and the general suspicion of imperial expansion which arrogates to itself a manifest destiny under supernatural guidance have spoiled Aeneas for many American readers. He is expected by them to act with humanity and honor toward the lady he loved and compromised, and is condemned for not doing so. But Vergil's story cannot be approached as a piece of disengaged fiction. It was controlled by two historical facts: the existence of Rome and the great struggle in the third and second centuries B.C. between Rome and Carthage. The actions of Aeneas are delimited by these

two historical facts. He must found Rome and he must provoke the enmity of Carthage. Now Dido, nobly and sympa-
thetically conceived in the spirit of the tragic heroine of
classical Greece and the pseudo-tragic heroine of Alexandrine
Greece, must also conform with the tradition of her rôle by
suffering and enmeshing herself in a tragic fate. Both the historical and literary tradition of Vergil inexorably set the mold
of his story for him. Both Aeneas and Vergil, so far as Dido
personally is concerned, would have preferred the realm of
pure fiction to the historical and literary delimitations under
which they had to operate. Vergil was somewhat cramped by
the demands of his story, but in using it he still reveals a keen
sympathy with the conflict imposed by the situation upon
Aeneas and Dido. Aeneas goes to Italy against his will, but
he goes and leaves Dido to her own undoing. Thus Vergil leads
one into the mystery of human suffering, which is caused at
times by a destiny which "knows not how to grow gentle under
human entreaties," and at times by well-meaning victims of
some tragic flaw or of their own tragic earnestness.

Vergil's organizing ability may be seen in his rearrangement of the episodes of Laocoön, the wooden horse, and Sinon.
As these episodes apparently existed in the epic cycle, the
Trojans took the horse into the city *before* determining what
disposition to make of it; Sinon was taken prisoner *while* they
were taking the horse into the city; and Laocoön and one of
his sons were slain by snakes *afterwards.* Vergil subordinates
the episodes of both Laocoön and Sinon to the all-important
problem of *whether* the horse should be taken in, combining
them and the wavering judgments of the Trojans into a dramatic series of curves of rising and falling action leading finally
to the logically correct but fatal decision that the horse should
be admitted. The originality of Vergil in this rearrangement,
however, must not be overstressed, since we have no way of

knowing the content of those intermediary sources which lay between the epic cycle and himself.

Vergil's task was to bring Aeneas—a synthesis of many true Roman qualities—through the fall of Troy without the stigma of cowardice and inaction, and to link his escape with a larger plan of Providence for the building of greater things. This he does by stressing the unscrupulous cunning of the Greeks as contrasted with the ingenuous credulity of the Trojans and the utter futility of opposing the manifest will of the gods. Aeneas set himself against the tide and flaunted death at every turn, but when the storm was over, he was part of the surviving human wreckage out of which was to be built a stronger nation in the West. Vergil's desire to vindicate Aeneas of the rôle probably attributed to him in previous Greek accounts of the fall of Troy will account for his omission of such details as the departure of Aeneas immediately after the Laocoön episode, the treacherous betrayal of country by Antenor (of whom Aeneas was, after the time of Vergil, and probably before also, regarded as an accomplice) the escape of Antenor, the capture of Aeneas and Andromache by Neoptolemus, the consent of the Greeks to the departure of Aeneas, and his choice of what he would save out of the fall of Troy. That Vergil did not mention the death of Astyanax and the sacrifice of Polyxena may be accounted for easily, if need be, in the fact that Aeneas tells of only those events which he himself saw. Vergil knew well enough his indebtedness to those in the past who had given artistic expression to this oft-told tale; but he could scarcely have imagined in the centuries that lay ahead, or in times when the reality of Troy was known no longer, the far-flung tradition, even among the uneducated, of the story of Troy's fall.[33]

Ovid preserves the unbroken continuity of the Trojan legend, but he brings to it the particular enthusiasms and limitations of his own personality. In the *Heroides* we have

41

a series of epistles—in effect, tragic monologues—written mostly by love-torn heroines of legend who are familiar to all of us. There are letters of Penelope to Odysseus, Briseis to Achilles, Oenone to Paris, Laodamia to Protesilaus, Paris to Helen, and Helen to Paris. Ovid has reinterpreted these legendary heroines in the light of his own sentimental and erotic interests. Heroic stature gives way to tragic pathos when Ovid is at his best; and when he is not, to rhetorical cleverness and facility. In the subtle feminine psychology, the Parisian suggestion of intrigue pervading all human relations, the sophistication and the glorification of subjective eroticism we see a projection of the Ovidian *demi-monde* into legends of the heroic past. In this way the past manages to live on in a real sense into the sophisticated, pleasure-loving, naughty, and thoroughly delightful world for which Ovid wrote.

In the twelfth and thirteenth books of the *Metamorphoses* Ovid again devotes himself to the Trojan War. After Homer and Vergil, these pages seem lifeless. The epic spirit of the great masters has evaporated, for which a certain sketchy rapidity (one could almost change the "r" to a "v") must suffice. The vividness of Homer and the depth of Vergil have disappeared, leaving a distinctly two-dimensional effect. The telescoping of practically the entire Trojan War into a series of stories told by the voluble Nestor over his cups at dinner to the chiefs, coming as it does virtually on the heels of the *Aeneid*, seems like nothing short of parody. We shall see as we proceed that our legend must lose something when interpreted in the arts of miniature. It might safely be inferred that the sleep which came over the chieftains within three verses after the golden words of Nestor had stopped was as welcome as it was swift. Almost half of the thirteenth book of the *Metamorphoses* is taken up with a rhetorical showpiece written strictly according to rule on the contest of Ajax and Odysseus for the arms of Achilles. Much of the traditional mythology of the Trojan War is introduced by the two heroes in support of their respective causes. After this model of rhetorical form comes a description of the fall of Troy and the wanderings of Aeneas.

Ovid's description of the fall of Troy shows him at his rare best. Rising into the realm of genuine pathos he relates the horror of the burning city and particularly the anguish of the women. We may see, among the other familiar scenes of Troy's fall, Hecuba amid the tombs of her sons, her seizure by Odysseus as she bore the ashes of her son Hector in her bosom and left a humble offering on his tomb. In describing the death of Polyxena, Ovid again rises above himself. His description of her nobility in the shadow of death is worthy of Greek tragedy, in whose spirit it is written. Equally tender is the lament of Hecuba over her fallen daughter.

## Latin Writers of the Early Empire

In the Empire, under the name of the younger Seneca, ten tragedies have survived. Of these the *Trojan Women* and the *Agamemnon* carry on the epic tradition of Troy in Latin tragedy. Were it not for the fact that the Greek tradition was destined soon to go into total eclipse, one might wistfully regret the far cry from the Homeric and tragic originals to their counterparts in Seneca. In place of the great creations in Greek epic and tragedy have come in Seneca frigid declamation, wearisome rant, and dramatic sterility, relieved by an occasionally pretty lyric or dramatic flash. The writers of the Empire as time went on found increasing consolation and refuge in the art of saying harmless things well. One might use regarding the whole period of post-Augustan literature the sentence of the younger Pliny regarding the poet Silius Italicus: *Scribebat carmina maiore cura quam ingenio.* The price of survival of our epic heroes was that they be recast in the patterns of thought and action of this different age. Ironically and sadly enough, Greek tragedy was destined to have as its principal carrier through the Middle Ages and down into the Renaissance the tragedies of Seneca. The price was great, was fated to be greater, but withal our story moves on. Also ascribed to the first century of our era is an anonymous abridgment of the *Iliad* in Latin, the *Ilias Latina,* a work of 1070 verses probably to be attributed to P. Baebius Italicus.[34] Though a work of only minor importance, still, through its use as a text, it carried on the tradition of Troy into the Middle Ages, a time when the ability to use Greek lay beyond the capacities of the West. An *Achilleis* of the first-century epic poet Statius also survives in fragmentary form. Apuleius in the second century describes in the tenth book of his *Metamorphoses,* with his usual intoxicating and sensual fullness, a pageant depicting the judgment of Paris. The scene was on an artificial hill representing Mt. Ida, which later was to disappear beneath the ground by some mechanical contrivance. A fountain stood ready to spray wine, colored with saffron, over the goats, and to carry its sweet perfume to the spectators, too. After the golden apple was presented to Venus, Hera and Athena went off angry and vowing revenge on Paris.[35]

### GREEK WRITERS OF THE EAST

In the East five writers of indifferent literary ability testify to the continued interest in the Trojan legend in the lengthening shadows of the late Roman Empire and in the Middle Ages: the Philostratus of the third century who probably came from Lemnos; Quintus of Smyrna, probably of the fourth century; Tryphiodorus, probably an Egyptian Greek of the middle of the fifth century; Colluthus, an Egyptian of the late fifth century;[36] and Tzetzes, born about 1110 in Constantinople. All of them wrote in Greek.

# THE LEGEND IN LITERATURE

PHILOSTRATUS.—The *Heroicus* of Philostratus is in the form of a dialogue between a Phoenician sea-faring traveler and a Thracian vinedresser. The vinedresser, seated under spreading trees in his vineyard on the shores of the Hellespont and not far from the tomb of the Greek hero Protesilaus, tells the stranger stories of heroes of the Trojan War which he learned from visits with the ghost of Protesilaus. In this work a note familiar to the Middle Ages is sounded, namely, one of reproof of Homer for mixing fact with fiction and distorting the real importance of heroes great with small. Philostratus tries to restore to importance heroes neglected by Homer and makes the old legends sometimes moral and sometimes what to his mind was dramatic.

QUINTUS OF SMYRNA.—Quintus in his *Posthomerica* of fourteen books tells in Homeric language the story of Troy from the burial of Hector, where the *Iliad* closes, down to the shipwreck of the Greek heroes (on their return home) at the hands of Athena and Poseidon. In his hands the legend of Troy's fall reverts in part to its characteristic Greek form. Vergil's central thesis of the divinely appointed mission of Rome is lacking in Quintus' account as a central thesis, just as is his artistic technique and good taste; though Quintus, being a part of the late Roman Empire, pays tribute to the heroism and piety of Aeneas and to the destiny and universality of Rome, and leans rather heavily on the directing power of the gods.[37] Those visible symptoms of greatness which haunt the pages of Homer and Vergil are absent here in Quintus. Realism takes the place of imaginative creativeness and the higher truth, and undoubtedly was a comforting substitute for them. The sources of Quintus' version cannot be definitely established, but they surely included some of the traditional pre-Vergilian literature.

In the eleventh book Aeneas stands as a mighty bulwark of

defense for Troy against the oncoming Greeks. Out of reverence for Aphrodite, Thetis turns Neoptolemus away from Aeneas. Shortly thereafter Aphrodite casts a thick mist around her son and to insure his safety takes him from the fray being enacted outside the walls. He then makes a no less valiant stand on the walls of his falling city.

The twelfth book relates the stratagem of the wooden horse. Quintus describes in detail the building of the horse. Epeus, its builder and the last man to climb in, pulls the ladder up after him. Knowing the mechanics of the bolt, he sits by it, whereas in Homer's reference to the horse in the *Odyssey* it was Odysseus who had charge of the operation of the door.[38] The Trojans find the horse and Sinon at the same time. Without equivocation they proceed from questions to threats and mutilation of Sinon, cutting off his ears and nose. Sinon tells his story briefly. Laocoön advises the burning of the horse, whereupon Athena strikes him mad and blind. The horse is then led into the city with festive pomp. When Laocoön continues to urge its destruction, Athena sends against his sons two serpents to destroy them. Cassandra plays her usual rôle and meets her usual fate.

In the thirteenth book Sinon signals to the Greeks at Tenedos with a torch and then summons his comrades from the horse. They descend by ladders. Far-flung pandemonium and slaughter ensue, which Quintus describes in great detail. Priam resignedly pleads for death when Neoptolemus approaches him. With but a few manly words Neoptolemus decapitates him. Antenor alone is spared, because of his former hospitality to Menelaus. Aeneas had been stubbornly fighting throughout the city, but when he sees destruction on every side, he sets his heart on escape. Placing his father on his broad shoulders and taking his son by the hand he flees, guided and protected by Aphrodite. Even Calchas bids the Greeks forbear, revealing the will of the gods that Aeneas should found a holy city on the Tiber and be revered among men of future generations, and rule—both himself and his illustrious descendants—over men of many tongues. Calchas also commends him for his piety to father and son. Menelaus slays Deiphobus; then tracing Helen, who had fled to the inner recesses of the palace, he would have slain her, had not Aphrodite cast a spell over him.

The fourteenth book of Quintus relates the departure of the Greeks. In a touching but revolting scene Polyxena is sacrificed. While the Greek fleet sails over the horizon, the pathetic captive women in tears and misery catch their last view of their native city—in flames.

TRYPHIODORUS.—Tryphiodorus is the author of *The Sack of Ilium,* a poem of 691 hexameters. Little is known of him, but Suidas informs us of the curious fact that in the *Odyssey* of Tryphiodorus each book entirely lacked the particular letter by which that book was denoted, the first book (A) lacking the letter alpha, the second book (B) lacking beta, et cetera; and that the author was a grammarian and epic poet. We might accept him as a grammarian. He, too, gives us an elaborate description of the wooden horse, part by part. The gods, as one might expect in a work of this time, have become rather bossy. While Sinon plays his usual rôle in this text, Laocoön does not appear at all. Under the crafty persuasion of Aphrodite, Helen would have betrayed the Greeks inside the horse by impersonating the voices of their wives, had not Odysseus constrained those within from answering and had not Athena on the outside led Helen off. During the night both Sinon and Helen signal by torchlight to the Greeks, the former beside the tomb of Achilles and the latter from the roof of her chamber. Spiriting away Anchises and Aeneas Aphrodite establishes them in Italy. In accordance with the will of the gods, says Tryphiodorus, imperishable sovereignty was thus established as the lot of the children of Aphrodite. The children and stock of Antenor, too, are spared in return for the hospitality of the former host of Odysseus and Menelaus. To orthodox Greek elements in his story Tryphiodorus has added the tradition of the building of Roman civilization out of the ashes of Troy, which was of primary interest to Rome, though, of course, not of Roman origin.[39]

COLLUTHUS and TZETZES.—The poem of Colluthus, *The Rape of Helen,* a work of 394 hexameters, was discovered, as was also the manuscript of Quintus, in Calabria in southern Italy. It tells the story of Paris and Helen from its inception at the wedding of Peleus and Thetis down to the arrival of the couple at Troy. Joannes Tzetzes, approximately a contemporary of Benoit in another distant part of the world, wrote an *Iliaca* divided into three parts: the *Antehomerica, Homerica,* and *Posthomerica.* This work of 1676 hexameters begins with the birth of Paris and continues down to the fall of Troy and the departure of the Greeks. The first of the parts includes the abduction of Helen and the assembling of the Greek expedition; the second part corresponds with the *Iliad;* and the third part includes the building of the wooden horse and the destruction of Troy. The sources of Tzetzes' *Posthomerica* were Quintus of Smyrna, Malalas, and Tryphiodorus. Behind all of these minor writers of the East undoubtedly lie sources now entirely lost.

## DICTYS AND DARES

The closing in of horizons and the decline of Greek in the West, which accompanied the dissolution of the Roman Empire, imposed upon the Trojan story strange conditions. The poems of the cyclic epic of early Greece were lost, and were never to be recovered. Homer and Troy along with him

Caricature of flight of Aeneas. Mural, Herculaneum.
Courtesy of the Yale University Press. See page 92

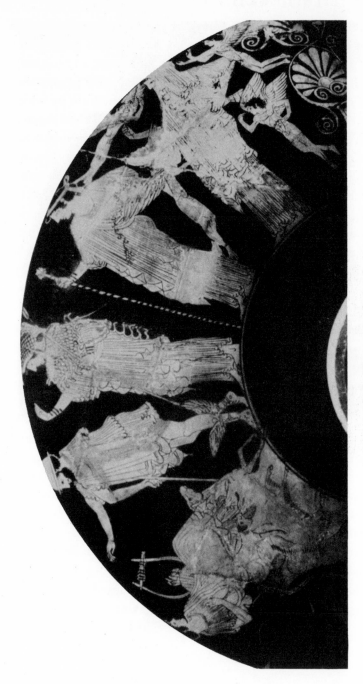

Judgment of Paris. Hieron *cylix*. Berlin. See page 97

survived in the cultural memory of the West largely through works of Graeco-Roman decadence, and under a guise which totally obliterated the spirit of the original poet and his song. Two intriguing Latin works the credentials and provenance of which are clothed in mystery served as a medium by which Troy entered into and survived through the Middle Ages in the West: the *Ephemeris*[40] *Belli Troiani* surviving under the name of Dictys of Crete, and the *De Excidio Troiae Historia*, a much shorter work of about thirty pages, under the name of Dares the Phrygian. The extant Latin version of Dictys, belonging probably to the fourth century of our era, carries the name of a Lucius Septimius, who states that the text which he herewith has translated was found in Dictys' tomb in Cnossus in Crete after the tomb had collapsed from age. This text, written by Dictys, a companion of Idomeneus in the Trojan War, in Phoenician characters upon the bark of a linden tree, was transcribed into Greek, according to Septimius, and presented to Nero. The suspicion generally entertained that some kind of Greek text actually lay behind the Latin version of Septimius has been confirmed by the discovery of a fragment of one belonging to the third century of our era and containing the substance of a part of the extant Latin version.[41] Beginning with the death of Atreus and the abduction of Helen, Dictys devoted five books to the history of the Trojan War. The remaining books of the original version, which related to the adventures of the Greek heroes on their return to their homes, thus continuing beyond the story of Dares, Septimius in his translation reduced to a single book of a few pages closing with the death of Odysseus.

The work of Dares carries with it a similar legend. Homer mentions a Trojan priest of Hephaestus named Dares,[42] and Aelian in the third century of our era states that there was extant in his time an *Iliad* of Dares.[43] This Dares, a participant in the Trojan War as an ally of the Trojans, was supposed to have recorded in Greek the history of the fall of Troy long before the time of Homer. In a letter which prefaces the Latin version of the supposed Greek original of Dares a Cornelius Nepos, dedicating the work to Sallustius Crispus, professes to have found at Athens the *History* of Dares written in the very hand of Dares, and to have faithfully translated it into Latin without making any changes in it. As has been said, the true history of this document will probably never be known. It may come out of the sixth century of our era. It can be understood in the light of the abundant romancing fiction, Greek and Latin, which in the twilight of the pagan world passed as history. Both the Nepos and the Sallust of the prefatory letter belonged to the first century B.C. Neither could have been guilty of the crude and barbaric Latin of this text or would have felt honored by having such a text associated with him. Moreover, one would hardly expect a document of this kind with its aspersions on the character of Aeneas and its denial of his mission to come out of either Latin or Greek literature of the Empire, for both were written under the spell of Rome. Yet the field of Greek fiction with its un-restrained inventiveness, its unending episodic monotony, its claims to historical authenticity, and its comparative freedom from the influence of Rome could have originated some document which would serve as a source for the Latin text which we have. The story of Dares begins with the Argonautic ex-pedition of the Greeks and ends with the sacrifice of Polyxena and the dispersal of the Greeks and Trojans assembled at Troy. Since the sympathy of the mediaeval reader generally lay with the Trojans to the extent that even down into the Renaissance there was a premium on Trojan lineage among the royal families of Europe, a preference was felt for Dares as a Trojan ally.

Both of these late Latin works professed in the original versions which they represented to relate either the personal experiences of the authors or verbal reports from the participants themselves of the Trojan War, and to precede Homer. Upon this basis they were accepted by the Middle Ages and down into the sixteenth century as giving a more reliable account of the Trojan legend than did Homer. Thus Baron Münchausen had at least two significant predecessors in antiquity. As the ability to read Greek passed away, these works were substituted for and, indeed, preferred to Homer. The absence in them of one of the crowning glories of Homer— the participation of divinities in the affairs of men—was accepted as a virtue. The decay of any real faith in these polytheistic conceptions in the Roman Empire and the triumph of the Christian faith brought to a close a tradition which had flourished from Homer to Vergil. The rationalization of the supernatural and the romantic treatment of women found in these two works are important forerunners of similar pronounced traits in the mediaeval legends of Troy. It is not necessary or even possible to think that Dictys and Dares held the field uncontested in their own times and as sources for future times. The name and fame of Vergil are written large in the annals of the centuries which separate him from Dante. The text of the *Aeneid* was generally available and widely used, though the second book, which links Troy to Rome, is not as important as others in the mediaeval tradition of Vergil. There is also the *Ilias Latina,* which served as a text in the schools for many centuries. Besides, translations and adaptations of classical texts often were made for the laity. And so, the existence of manuscripts presenting a tradition different from that given by Dictys and Dares suggests the probability of there having been available in the Middle Ages some orthodox Latin account of the Trojan legend deriving from the ancient authors.[44] But such an independent tradition lacked the prestige and the appeal to interfere with or displace the tradition of Dictys and Dares.

DICTYS' ACCOUNT OF THE FALL OF TROY.—The Latin versions of the works of Dictys and Dares presented to the Middle Ages a version of the fall of Troy that was materially different in spirit from those heretofore outlined, although it seems certain that such a tradition must have existed at least in late Greek times. The tincture of time and the will of Rome have probably combined to eradicate it. Dictys developed the story of a serious defection of the Trojan elders from Priam and his pro-Paris policy. Antenor, with Aeneas as an accomplice, becomes the spokesman for an appeasement policy; and Priam, proud and hated king, has to accede to the pressure brought upon him to close the war. In their parleys with the Greeks Antenor and Aeneas betray their city into the hands of the enemy. Agamemnon, Idomeneus, Odysseus, and Diomedes constitute a secret embassy of the Greeks to bargain with Antenor. It is agreed that should Aeneas wish to enter into the collusion, a part of the booty would be his, and his whole household would be spared; whereas Antenor himself would have half of the wealth of Priam and the throne would be given to that one of his sons whom he should choose. The actual report of progress of Antenor upon his return to Troy was far different from what had actually happened. The terms which he brought back were designed to betray Troy into the hands of the Greeks, as, for example, that the Greeks should present a gift to Minerva and be willing upon receipt of Helen and an indemnity to bring the war to a close and return home. With matters of foreign policy taken out of the hands of Priam, Antenor and Aeneas are sent back to the Greek chieftains for another parley. Before they set out, Helen comes to Antenor secretly in the middle of the night, suspecting that she is to be handed over to Menelaus and fearing the consequences of her infidelity. She asks Antenor to plead for her and to say that she had hated Troy after the death of Paris and wanted to return home. This message Antenor and Aeneas convey. Diomedes sets an indemnity with peremptory brusqueness, and Panthus asks for a day's grace for deliberation regarding it. Meanwhile Antenor, through a combination of persuasion, force, and promises, induces his wife Theano, who was also the priestess of the temple of Minerva, to entrust him with the Palladium, upon the presence of which in the city the safety of Troy depends. He then delivers it to the Greeks. Also, a slightly lower indemnity than had originally been asked is agreed upon.

With these arrangements made, the story proceeds to the betrayal of the city along the lines secretly planned by the Greek chiefs. The Greeks decide that a gift must be presented to Minerva to bring her the greatest possible honor. Helenus, who already had thrown himself suppliantly at the mercy of the Greeks when he foresaw the imminent danger of the Trojan cause,[45] informs the Greeks that the doom of Troy was sealed now that the Palladium had been removed from the city, and that the gift to Minerva in the form of a wooden horse large enough to necessitate the breaking of the wall was fatal for the Trojans. On hearing this, Achilles' son puts Helenus under armed guard in order that this information may not be disclosed to the enemy. The peace pact is solemnly ratified amid rejoicing on both sides. The Trojans extol Antenor with the highest praise and worship him as a god for having brought peace to their city. Meanwhile the wooden horse is constructed under the supervision of Epeus. It is to be used not as a hiding place for Greek warriors, but merely as a means of providing an entrance into the city through the broken wall.[46] The indemnity of gold and silver agreed upon is placed, amid

the highest enthusiasm, under the direction of Antenor and
Aeneas, in the temple of Minerva. Carrying out the subterfuge
with scrupulous care, the Greeks enter into the spirit of
peace by refraining from any act of warfare. The horse is
piously accepted by the Trojans. But finding that the gates
of the city impeded them they tear down part of the city wall.
The Greeks now insist on actually receiving the indemnity
before the horse is led inside the wall. Odysseus assembles the
Trojan workmen to repair the Greek fleet in anticipation of
a speedy departure, and amid merriment and festal joy Trojan
men and women vie with one another in bringing the horse
into their city.

Setting fire to their tents the Greeks now sail to Sigeum,
there to wait for nightfall. While the Trojans are relaxed in
drunken slumber after the celebration of the peace, the Greeks
sail back to the city, watching for the fire signal of Sinon, who
had been secretly placed for that very purpose. His rôle is
one of action and not of words. There is no place for fine
rhetoric in this bare account of Dictys. Once inside the city
the Greeks carry out the traditional slaughter and pillage,
which need not be repeated. The homes of Antenor and Aeneas
alone are spared in the sack of the city. Priam flees to the altar
of Jupiter, but to no avail. Cassandra is likewise dragged from
sanctuary. Deiphobus is horribly disfigured and then slain
by Menelaus. Ajax wants to have Helen slain, but Menelaus,
his love for her still lingering on, by canvassing and pleading
with the chieftains, one by one, prevails upon them to spare
her life. This purely rational version of the disposition of
Helen differs from that of Quintus of Smyrna, in whose account Aphrodite casts a spell over Menelaus in order to pre-
vent him from slaying Helen. When Hecuba flies off into a
tantrum of imprecations against the Greeks, she is stoned to
death. This, too, is a rationalization of the usual form of the

legend, that she is turned into a dog, as found, for example, in Euripides' *Hecuba*. Ajax, Odysseus, and Diomedes all want the Palladium, but when Odysseus flees in fear at the finding of Ajax murdered, the Palladium goes to the only survivor of the three, Diomedes. The Greeks urge Aeneas to sail to Greece with them, promising him a kingdom on equal terms with themselves. But he remains at Troy, and after the departure of the Greeks he tries, but to no avail, to enlist neighboring allies in a conspiracy to drive Antenor from the throne. Antenor discovers this plot, and consequently Aeneas is barred from Troy. So sailing away to the Adriatic he founds Corcyra Melaena (Curzola). Antenor, remaining in control at Troy, enjoys the love and respect of all.

As is obvious in the preceding summary, the whole thesis which Vergil built into the *Aeneid* is ignored in this late version of the fall of Troy.[47] The very essence of great epic—the noble and ennobling deeds of men wrought by themselves at the expense of great toil, self-sacrifice, and heroism—but with the help of Heaven—is contemptuously ignored in Dictys' account. On the contrary, the traitorous Aeneas, finally enmeshed in machinations against his fellow conspirator, is forced to sail away to a destiny of no significance. We have passed, as it were, from the inspired exaltation of grand opera to the smallness of the ordinary stage. This is not the spirit even of late Roman, but of decadent Greek literature. Needless to say, the style, the superb artistic technique of organization in terms of climax and catastrophe, the interrelation of outer action and inner forces, and the character portrayal found in Vergil are missing here. Nor will anything better be found in Dares.

DARES' ACCOUNT OF THE FALL OF TROY.—The considerably shorter Latin version of Dares' account of the fall of Troy bears certain differences from and similarities to the account of Dictys. A point of resemblance in the two versions is the fact that Antenor heads a conspiracy to betray his city, and takes Aeneas into his confidence. Together they open the Scaean gate at night to admit Neoptolemus and his forces. This obviates the need for the wooden horse. Sinon, however, is mentioned, as he is in Dictys, too. When Agamemnon shares all the booty with his army, Antenor and Aeneas have their property restored as recompense for their services to the Greeks. Meeting Hecuba and Polyxena in flight Aeneas hides the latter in the home of his father. When Antenor is pressed to release Polyxena, upon discovering her at the home of Anchises, he hands her over to Agamemnon. Without further delay she is then given over to Neoptolemus for slaughter. Angry at Aeneas for hiding Polyxena, Agamemnon orders him to depart forthwith from the land. This Aeneas does, setting out with a following of thirty-four hundred people in the twenty-two ships in which Paris had gone to Greece. Antenor remains at Troy.

Widely divergent as were the accounts of the fall of Troy in Vergil on the one hand and in Dictys and Dares on the other, yet both accounts were available to the Middle Ages. That this mediaeval version of Aeneas' activities, if it had any vogue in classical antiquity, was unable seriously to compete with the orthodox version in Greek and Roman antiquity is obvious in the almost complete absence of reference to it in classical literature and in the total absence of it in the surviving traditions of the other arts. If the accounts of Vergil and of Dictys and Dares were used in different spheres, their divergence need not have caused any sharp controversy. The point of conflict, at all events, was not an important one to the mediaeval mind. The evident ennobling of Aeneas in Vergil's account did not appeal, at least to the popular mediaeval mind, as strongly as the stylistic plainness and the elements of romance which invited development in the stories of Dictys and Dares.

## MEDIAEVAL ACCOUNT OF TROJAN ORIGIN OF FRANKS

A striking development of the Trojan legend during the Middle Ages was the belief in the Trojan origin of the Franks. This "historical" thesis is advanced by Fredegarius Scholasticus of the middle of the seventh century in his *Chronicle* written in a Burgundian monastery. His version of the story is that part of the Trojan exiles with their wives and children went to Europe with their king, Francio; they occupied one bank of the Rhine, and not far from the Rhine tried to build a replica of Troy, though their work remained unfinished. After their king they were called Franci.[48] A charter of Dagobert I, King of the Franks and patron of Fredegarius, also recognizes this tradition of the origin of his people. It is to be hoped that the reliability of Fredegarius' story is further above reproach than his Latin, which is barbarous; but when one reads in his narrative that Priam (!) carried off Helen, one has misgivings about both. A brief document purporting to be a *History* of the Phrygian Dares on the origin of the Franks names at the close of his account of the Trojan War a Franco from whom the Franks derived their name and ancestry.[49] Another mediaeval document (of the eighth century) called *Liber Historiae Francorum,* brings Aeneas to Italy after the fall of Troy. Other Trojan chiefs, among them Priam and Antenor, went with their people to the banks of the Don River and finally reached Pannonia (Hungary) by the sea of Azov, where they began to build a city called Sicambria. At this juncture the rebellious race of the Alani, conquered by the Roman emperor Valentinian, fled to the sea of Azov. When the Emperor promised a large reward to any who should dislodge the Alani from that region, the Trojans with the Romans drove them out. Because of their resolute courage in this venture the Emperor called the Trojans "Franci," assuming some resemblance between this word and *feri* ("wild").[50] Geoffrey of Monmouth in the twelfth century also postulated a Trojan origin for England. Britain was supposed to have been founded by and named from Brutus of the line of Aeneas. This tradition survived into the sixteenth century.[51]

## Benoit de Sainte Maure

Though the literary merits of the Latin versions of Dictys and Dares are negligible, their influence upon the epic romances of mediaeval Europe both in the East and West and upon the Renaissance was far reaching. The *Roman de Troie* of Benoit de Sainte Maure is the most important work of this type. A discursive epic romance of some thirty thousand verses, longer than both the *Iliad* and *Odyssey* combined, and attributed to the years 1160-1165, it relates the story of Troy in an encyclopedic way *ab ovo*, starting with the winning of the golden fleece by Jason in his Argonautic expedition, passing on to the first Greek expedition against Laomedon's Troy under the direction of Heracles, the second Trojan War familiar to all of us, the return of the Greek heroes to their homes, and ending with the death of Odysseus at the hands of Telegonus, his son by Circe. Here we have an important product of the Renaissance of the twelfth century. In all but the story it is a true child of its time. Looking at the Homeric picture, completely distorted as it was by the limitations of his sources, Dictys and Dares, and by the flickering light of his own day, Benoit with the transforming eye of a child saw in it the familiar reflection of his own age. He had no equipment to re-create the environment or even to understand the language of the Homeric originals. With an Ovidian magic the mind of the twelfth century transformed a legend of ancient Greece into the realities of contemporary life in France. Customs, religion, clothing and furniture, military arms and tactics, and architecture are all part of French feudal life. Kings, cavaliers, barons, dukes, princes, and vassals walk through the pages of Benoit. In order to survive in any real way, the ancient heroes had to take on the protective coloring of their new environment. The pagan temple became through magic metamorphosis the Christian cathedral, just as in Ovid a humble cottage became a temple for Philemon and Baucis. Calchas changed from a priest into a bishop. Since this was a civilized age, it readily engaged in warfare, though it undoubtedly disapproved of it. Men, in those days gallant and chivalrous, were quick to avenge their outraged ladies, and it seems to follow, to outrage them. Hector is the *beau idéal* of the time, being vigorous, courageous, patriotic, liberal, self-sacrificing, moderate of counsel, and not indifferent to the praise of ladies. War and love are the poles which magnetize these mediaeval heroes and heroines into action. The age of the Crusades saw in the story of Troy an image of its own absorbing interests. Since the Trojans were supposed to have founded many colonies in the West after the sack of Troy, they were held in greater esteem than the Greeks. The ennoblement of Hector at the expense of Achilles, therefore, was natural in Benoit's story. Achilles is called a faithless coward. From the literary point of view this work has caught both the virtues and the shortcomings of its time. Sweetness and naive charm on the one hand are counterbalanced on the other by inexcusable diffuseness, redundance, lack of dramatic relief, and (with the virtual disappearance of the supernatural) lack of epic perspective.[52]

Dictys' and Dares' accounts of the fall of Troy (according to Benoit's own testimony) were used by him in the *Roman de Troie*. The tradition of the duplicity of Antenor, called the pagan Judas, and Aeneas, called by Hecuba a Satan, in betraying their city is preserved in this French novel. They felt that Priam should have returned Helen to the Greeks. Indignant, Priam conspired against their lives; whereupon they decided to betray their city into the hands of the enemy. Many of the details of Dictys' story reappear in the *Roman de Troie,* including the theft of the Palladium, the episode of the wooden horse, and the signal from Sinon. The familiar outrages attendant upon the fall of Troy recur.[53] Antenor had Aeneas exiled for having concealed Polyxena when she was being hunted for sacrifice. Aeneas, accepting his destiny, reassembled the surviving Trojans and advised those who did not wish to follow him to accept the leadership of Antenor. But having learned after the departure of the Greeks that Antenor had brought about his exile by bribing the Greek chieftains, Aeneas determined to drive out Antenor. The latter, dissuaded by his friends from offering any resistance, thereupon sailed away and founded Corcyra Melaena in the Adriatic. There he was joined by eleven vessels of Trojans left at Troy.[54]

TROILUS AND CRESSIDA, FROM HOMER TO DRYDEN.—The story of Troilus and Briseida in Benoit's work is beginning a long literary history of its own. The separation of the two lovers is already impending when their story opens in Benoit. Briseida, amorous coquette that she was, in arriving at the camp of the Greeks, where she had come to join her father, the seer Calchas, who had deserted the Trojans, made Diomedes her first conquest. This doughty hero survived his adversaries on the field of battle only to succumb to the shafts of Cupid. Tears, sighs, and laments harass the sleepless nights of Diomedes. In the same way Achilles, in Benoit's story, is stricken with a passion for Polyxena, comparing himself with the mythological Narcissus in not being able to have the object of his love.[55] The mediaeval warrior was also a lover—*militat omnis amans.* What with the revival of Ovid and the upwelling from within of new feelings of romantic love, no hero or heroine could afford to be slow of tongue or of mind. The heroine must listen attentively to the plaintive lover, and be nimble and ready in her reply. The caprices of the female heart offer a fruitful field for philosophizing, and the symptoms of love for elaboration. Beauty and chastity are pawns in the game of love. Beauty was much desired.[56] Briseida was well schooled for life, as shown in the description of her found in an Old French version of the *Roman de Troie* in prose, as follows:

> *Elle fu de mout grant biauté et de belle fachon et de grant maniere sage et bien parlans, et mout mist son cuer en amor.*
>
> She was a lady of exceeding beauty, highly stylish, sophisticated in bearing, and ready of tongue, and had her heart on love.

It seems opportune at this place before leaving the story of Troilus in literature to observe its historical continuity. The principal figures in this story—Pandarus, from whom is derived our English verb "to pander," Cressida, who has only her name in common with the Homeric Chryseis, and Troilus—are scarcely more than names in the *Iliad*. In the *Cypria* of the epic cycle, however, Troilus played a prominent rôle. In opposing Achilles he was slain. The slaying of Troilus by Achilles was also amply handled by Greek vase painters of early times, as we shall see in the chapter on ceramics. In the Latin version of Dictys[57] Troilus was slain in his early years of boyhood by order of Achilles. This version, therefore, fails to capitalize upon the dramatic or romantic possibilities of the story. But the Latin text of Dares elevated Troilus as a warrior to a position second only to Hector, whose death at the hands of Achilles[58] precedes the same doom destined soon to befall Troilus.[59] This version falls in line with the general

61

exaltation of Troilus into prominence by the *Cypria* and the mythological handbooks.[60] So it remained for Benoit to develop this story amid the shadows of Troy's last days. This he has done with real pathos. The heroine he called Briseida, a romantic, alluring person of Indian extraction, though she has nothing in common with Homer's Briseis. Boccaccio in his *Filostrato* found the ill-starred love of Troilus for the unfaithful Criseida, by which name the heroine is now known, a mold into which he might pour his own passionate but unhappy love for the immortal Fiammetta. In this demonstration of erotic psychology Troilus the warrior becomes Troilus the lover. Chaucer's *Troilus and Criseyde,* written a half century later, shows its author at the peak of his power in the field of sustained narration. The immediate and main inspiration of Chaucer's *Troilus* was Boccaccio's *Filostrato,* but his story is rich with the spoils of Time and with the largeness of Chaucer's own skill and philosophical reflection. Pandarus, in Boccaccio's version the cousin of Criseida, has become in Chaucer's the uncle of the same heroine, with an accompanying complexity of character. Chaucer's Criseyde likewise has grown out of the psychological simplicity of Boccaccio's creation into a more complex and subtle character. Shakespeare found the principal elements of his *Troilus and Cressida* in Chaucer's story, in the English prose version of Lefèvre's *Receuil des Histoires de Troyes* published by Caxton, and possibly in Homer's *Iliad.* His realistic and cynical portrayal of the faithless Cressida, who forsook Troilus for Diomedes, before she had time to tire of the one or know the other, carries one beyond the versions of both Boccaccio and Chaucer, and has made Cressida a byword for wantonness and infidelity.[61] Dryden in his *Troilus and Cressida,* published in 1679, redeemed the good name of Cressida from the stigma attached to it in Shakespeare's play. Her infidelity with Diomedes is part of her ruse to enable her and her father to return to Troy. When reproached by Troilus she forfeits her own life in the best tragic tradition. No useful end was served by Dryden's rehandling of Shakespeare's story except that it led Dryden to discover Chaucer and to reinstate him to his rightful place in English letters. As will be seen later, Morley in *The Trojan Horse* brings us a Troilus and Cressida in modern dress and environment.

## SPREAD OF TRADITION OF DICTYS, DARES, AND BENOIT OVER EUROPE

Benoit's romantic epic of the twelfth century had an influence down to the early seventeenth century that was equaled only by its own length. An indication of the lively appeal of the *Roman de Troie* lies in the twenty-eight manuscripts, all complete or nearly so, which have survived into modern times. With the disappearance of the Greek language from the West it was impossible for Benoit to consult the original text of Homer. Indeed, at the beginning of his poem he repudiates Homer in favor of Dictys and Dares, the former of whom serves as Benoit's only source after the death of Polyxena, the point where Dares' story closes. In Benoit's story, then, and in the works of Dictys and Dares, from which he derived it, we have the ultimate source of knowledge of the story of Troy, and often its principal carriers through the Middle Ages and down into the Renaissance. Their combined tradition ramified all through Europe. In them the Middle Ages made the classical legend genuinely its own.[62] Both the *De Bello Troiano* of Joseph of Exeter, written in Latin hexameters about the year 1188, a work known to Chaucer and praised by Milton, and the *Troilus* of Albert of Stade, written in Latin elegiacs and completed in 1249, are based upon the Latin text of Dares.

GUIDO DE COLUMNIS.—But the piece of Latin prose which exercised a far-flung influence throughout Europe is the *Historia Destructionis Troiae* of Guido de Columnis, a judge at Messina. This work, except for the first book, the author dashed off in the year 1287 in seventy-one days. With literary ethics as loosely defined as they were in those times it is not surprising to find this abridged paraphrase of Benoit's *Roman de Troie* not even mentioning Benoit, but referring glibly and disparagingly to Homer, whom the author could not have read, to Ovid, Vergil, Dictys, and Dares, the former of which pair he may have known only through Benoit. This work of Guido eclipsed its French model in popularity and became one of the most popular books of the Middle Ages. The Bibliothèque Nationale in Paris has more manuscripts of Guido than of Benoit. Guido's work went through eight printed editions in the early years of printing. Numerous translations of it were made in Italian, French, German, Spanish, Flemish, Scotch, Bohemian, and English. Its influence lived on of itself down to the beginning of the eighteenth century, as well as through Lydgate and Caxton.[63]

EUROPE IN GENERAL.—In Germany the tradition of Benoit lived on in the *Song of Troy (Liet von Troye)* of Herbort of Fritslâr and in the *Trojan War (Trojanischer Krieg)* of Konrad of Würzburg, both of the thirteenth century. The second of these German writers left his poem only half finished at his death. He had written only forty thousand verses! Herbort's poem, over eighteen thousand verses long, was composed in the period 1210-1217. He was acquainted with the *Metamorphoses, Art of Love,* and *Heroides* of Ovid, with Vergil and, in all likelihood, with the *Achilleis* of Statius. Herbort's work is a free rendering of that of Benoit. Love comes at first sight and man has a yearning instinct. Achilles, love-smitten, acts as though he had a toothache; Diomedes

Achilles outraging the body of Hector. *Lecythus.*
Courtesy of the Metropolitan Museum of Art, New York. See page 101

Priam entering the tent of Achilles. *Cotyle.* Vienna. See page 101

clings to his beloved as a fish to a hook. The curious blending of pagan with Christian is seen in the forecasting of the coming of Christ by the Sibyl Cassandra!

In France Jacques Milet through his *Destruction of Troy* (*Destruction de la Troie*) published in 1484, carried on, in length at least, and in general outline as well, the tradition of Benoit. Brevity being a virtue even among such masters of garrulity, he alone must serve as a symbol in fifteenth century France of a lively interest in the story of Troy. Similarly poems on the Trojan legend which come out of the tradition of Dictys, Dares, Benoit, and Guido, and which often revert to Vergil, Ovid, and Statius, may be found in abundance in Dutch, Italian, Greek, English, and even Icelandic. To the early English reader, for example, Troy was known through the *Troy Book* (1412-1420) of Lydgate, a much amplified version in verse of Guido's prose *History,* and through Caxton's *Recuyell,* published about 1474, which was a prose version of Lefèvre's *Receuil des Histoires de Troyes.* Lydgate's story, consisting of 30,117 lines, begins with the Argonautic expedition, meanders through the account of the fall of Laomedon's Troy, the labors of Hercules, the abduction of Helen in reprisal for the previous abduction of Laomedon's daughter Hesione, the diatribes of Guido against the wiles of woman, the author's studious defense of the fair sex, his expressed inability to match in English the descriptive powers of Guido in the area of a blueprint of Helen's beauty, mention of Statius, the lying Homer, Ovid, and Vergil, the authentic accounts of Dictys and Dares, compliments to Chaucer and Petrarch, high praise of Guido, digressions on false gods and idolatry, the mediaeval and non-Homeric version of the Trojan War, the varied fortunes of the surviving Greeks and Trojans, and a statistical analysis of the war. Caxton's book, his first venture as a publisher and the first book printed in

English, went through some twenty editions over a period of two and a half centuries.

## ITALIAN RENAISSANCE

The Italian Renaissance succeeded the Middle Ages with the same quivering energy and vibrant enthusiasm as adolescence comes to youth. Petrarch (1304-1374) at its beginning and Leo X (1513-1521) at its end are separated by almost two centuries. Its great foster child was the Revival of Learning, that is, revival of knowledge of its ancient Graeco-Roman past; and it undertook its work with the true enthusiasm and devotion of a mother. In the words of one of our poets:

> In vain we build the world unless
> The builder also grows.

The builders of the Renaissance grew at their task and discovered their best selves in the doing of it. It demanded much of them and gave more in return. Our greatest debt to the Renaissance lies in the broad base of culture which it laid as a foundation for further progress in our modern world. The Italian Renaissance was the most spontaneous and wholehearted in its absorption of Greek and Roman culture.

Dante, the last great flower of mediaevalism, was mediaeval in knowing no Greek. But for a century before the fall of Constantinople in 1453 Greek manuscripts had been coming into Italy. About the year 1354 Petrarch came into possession of a manuscript of Homer, though he could not read it. He soon acquired translations of Homer, and late in life learned some Greek. This was a difficult accomplishment, since no handbooks of the Greek language existed in either Latin or Italian. One had to learn ancient Greek from some learned Greek, who would have to be imported. Boccaccio (1313-1375) is the first Italian on record to make some progress with

66

ancient Greek. With Petrarch and Boccaccio came a renewed interest in Homer and Vergil from a more secular point of view. The Medici Library in Florence, opened in 1444, housed what was then the most complete classical library in existence. The *editio princeps* of Vergil was published about the year 1469. The *Aeneid* rose into undisputed prominence as an epic model. The *editio princeps* of Homer was made in 1488.

## RENAISSANCE OVER EUROPE

Having spent its force in Italy by the time of Leo X the Renaissance spread into France, Spain, Germany, the Netherlands, and England. The reaction of these countries to the new virus was different in each instance, but one thing is clear regarding it, that the over-all result of the vaccination was a modified native culture rather than, as in Italy, a modified ancient culture. In the wake of the publication of Greek texts came Latin translations of them. Erasmus (1466-1536) was the first to publish translations of Greek tragedy. The present writer has in his possession a translation of the *Iliad* in Latin by Andreas Divus of Justinopolis in Asia Minor. It is both refreshing and typical of the cosmopolitan character of the Renaissance to find a Greek from Asia Minor translating Homer into Latin from a Venetian text and publishing his work in Paris. For this translation of Homer was based upon the Aldine edition and was published in Paris in 1538. It reproduced the Aldine text verbatim in Latin, page for page and line for line, and may be regarded as an index of the current understanding of Homer by many readers and of the medium through which they had to approach Homer. The translation completely lacks literary style. In the foreword the translator states his intention "of expressing the lines of Homer as faithfully as possible, of not illuminating the lines of Homer with any added colors or adorning them with any

veneer, but of merely drawing the picture itself and of conforming to the truth as though it were reproduced with
carbon." His words are:

> . . . *lineamenta, quam fideliter possem, exprimerem, nullis
> illa coloribus illustrans, nullo fuco exornans, tantum imaginem
> ipsam ducens, ac veluti carbone notatam ad veritatem con
> formans.*

The publisher characterizes the book as designed to help the
reader in his studies with a view to making possible a quick
comparison of the Greek and Latin texts. A comparison of the
first two verses of the *Iliad* in the original and in this Latin
version will reveal the literalness of it and its total lack of
artistic qualities:

> Μῆνιν ἄειδε, θεά, Πηληιάδεω ᾽Αχιλῆος
> Iram cane, Dea, Pelidae Achillis

> οὐλομένην, ἣ μυρί᾽ ᾽Αχαιοῖς ἄλγε᾽ ἔθηκεν.
> pernitiosam, quae infinitos Achivis dolores inflixit.

European editions of Greek authors in the sixteenth and seventeenth centuries and later usually included a Latin translation
on the page facing the Greek text. Considerable familiarity
with Greek on the part of writers of the sixteenth century must
not be taken for granted.

## ELIZABETHAN ENGLAND

In England the popularity of the Trojan legend grew among
both the educated and the uneducated classes.[64] The early
Elizabethans found much of real value to themselves in the
heritage of classical mythology, and in this heritage the Trojan
legend because of its ancient prestige and undying beauty
remained a distinct favorite. The reading of pertinent parts of

later sections on the Trojan legend in painting and tapestry should leave with the reader a conception of the extent to which the story of Troy had penetrated into the popular consciousness and the arts all over Europe at this time.

EARL OF SURREY, PEELE, SACKVILLE, WARNER, MARLOWE. The interest of the Earl of Surrey (*c.* 1518-1547) in the Trojan legend may be traced back to his generous education in the Classics and Italian literature in his youth. He is sometimes thought of as the English Petrarch and as the father of modern English poetry, since he created English blank verse in his translation of both the second and the fourth books of the *Aeneid*. He fell a victim prematurely to the political rivalries of the day and was sentenced to be hanged, drawn, and quartered, though in reality he was subsequently only beheaded. There were those patriotic scholars or those novices who, like George Peele in his drama *The Arraignment of Paris* (1584) or *The Tale of Troy* (1589) the sources of which were Ovid and Vergil for the greater part of the story of Troy's fall and Caxton for the main plan of the poem,[65] reproduced in brief compass the accumulated tradition of the past. In the foreword to this latter work Peele recommends his work as a stimulus to the chivalry and the bravery of his countrymen. The story moves quickly from the birth of Paris to his participation in the award of the golden apple, the abduction of Helen, the Greek expedition to Troy, a passing tribute to Chaucer's *Troilus and Criseyde*, Hecuba's offer of Polyxena to Achilles, the death of Achilles at the hands of Paris, the building of the wooden horse, the stratagem of Sinon, the sack of the city, and the escape of Aeneas to Carthage and finally to Italy. There were the balladmakers singing of the wandering prince of Troy with a new moral seriousness and didactic virtuosity. There were those who, like Thomas Sackville in his *The Induction,* haunted by the insecurity of man's estate

69

and the uncertainty of fortune's favors, found in the fall of Troy an opportunity to develop that pervading obsession of the time. In this work of Sackville, Sorrow appeared to him and led him to the lower world; and his brief description of the fate of Troy comes in his account of the gloomy abode of that other world. There were finally those, such as William Warner, called the English Homer, who included an account of the Trojan War in his rhyming historical epic *Albion's England* (1586) and gratified contemporary interest in chivalry, romantic love, and England's early history as a supposed colony of Trojan lineage. Out of this period comes Marlowe's rapturous and adolescent apostrophe to Helen:

> Was this the face that launched a thousand ships,
> And burnt the topless towers of Ilium!
> Sweet Helen, make me immortal with a kiss.
> Her lips suck forth my soul! see where it flies;
> Come, Helen, come, give me my soul again;
> Here will I dwell, for heaven is in those lips,
> And all is dross that is not Helena.

> Oh thou art fairer than the evening air
> Clad in the beauty of a thousand stars.
>
> *Faustus*

SHAKESPEARE, HEYWOOD, CHAPMAN.—Shakespeare wove into his *Lucrece* a lengthy description with its many familiar details of the sack of Troy. The description is introduced through the device of a painting of which the heroine, recently violated by Tarquin, thinks as she awaits the arrival of her husband. Standing before the painting, like a true Alexandrine heroine she declaims, moralizes, and gushes. The Trojan story may also be found in such works of Thomas Heywood as the *Iron Age*, a version of the entire legend in dramatic form, and

*Troia Britanica* (1609) an inclusive chronicle from chaos to the accession of James I enshrining the idea of the early founding of Britain by the Trojans. Though in the dedication of this work the only authorities mentioned are Homer and Vergil, these authors—and Ovid as well—were used but little. For Caxton with his mediaeval tradition provided the main foundations of the work. Another product of this age is the first complete English translation of the *Iliad,* the work of George Chapman, which appeared during the years 1596-1611. This translation rises to the good, but not above the bad qualities of its age. The simplicity and directness of Homer are often lost in a cloud of pedantry, morality, and didacticism. But there is no doubting the genuineness of his love for Homer. Critical comments of editions of Homer used by Chapman find their way in moralized form into his translation. The translation of the last half of the *Iliad* Chapman executed in fifteen weeks. The age of Pope found this early translation especially distasteful, but to Keats and his circle Chapman and his age were once again to "speak out loud and bold." It may be of interest to observe in passing that the first complete American translation of the *Iliad* was not made for two and a half centuries after Chapman's translation, being that of the Virginian, Munford, and published in 1846.

## Seventeenth and Eighteenth Centuries

Behind the best thought of the seventeenth and eighteenth centuries lay the qualities of rationalism, skepticism, and inquisitiveness with regard to man and his institutions, to the universe and its operations, and to mechanical apparatus. Important steps were taken in exploring and inhabiting the universe and in reappraising commercially the world's goods and tangible resources in the light of a new situation. These two centuries witnessed a wholesome establishment of broader intellectual frontiers, elimination of mental wastelands and moral swamps, and at least one brave new social experiment in the new world on principles established in the political philosophy of ancient Greece and Rome. In this time also came a broad expansion of knowledge about classical antiquity and an extension of the facilities by which ancient literature and art could be understood at first hand. These centuries became the battleground on which the vested interests of a millennium now reaching its unprogressive decadence struggled to maintain themselves against a growing awareness of the startling possibilities of a new world built upon the foundations of classical antiquity and guided by the inventive skill of contemporary instruments.

Unfortunately, even the best qualities of this period were inadequate and unfair to life's will-o'-the-wisp hope of fulfillment of its total potentialities. An age of reason which disavows the guidance of the creative imagination and which spends its energies in exploiting the universe for commercial purposes falls far short of Plato's chariot of the mind guided upward by pure spirit. At least, the restoration to the western world of Homer and Vergil as readable texts guaranteed the continuance of the legend of Troy as it was in those texts, and dealt a deathblow to the tradition represented by Dictys, Dares, Benoit, and Caxton. The eighteenth century had its Pope as the seventeenth had its Dryden to confirm the ancient tradition of Homer and Vergil through their translations. Mythology, which once was set by Homer to the supreme order of organized dreaming, could hardly flourish, though it could survive, in an environment of unimaginative skepticism, deflating satire and travesty. The sportive and irreverent Rev. James Smith illustrates this trait of his time in his poem *The Innovation of Penelope and Ulysses* (1658). Just at the end of the eighteenth century (1797) there appeared a translation in burlesque of Homer by Thomas Brydges, which went into several editions. It is a curious satirical work with quaint woodcuts in the style of the pictorial artist Hogarth. But a worse enemy of the spirit of mythology than satire and travesty is the unimaginative approach of those whose cold touch embalms even before it kills. Hence the great bulk of unfeeling and frigid allusions to mythology which linger on even into the pages of Byron. Cowley, who at the age of ten could write an epical romance on Pyramus and Thisbe, lived to decry the outworn stories of Thebes and Troy. Milton, parenthetically, has the strength and the splendor which negates and truly measures the limitations of his time. But beginning with the latter half of the eighteenth century there appears in Germany and England a violent literary and artistic reaction against the formal, spiritually depressed, low-tensioned neoclassicism which had been currently in vogue. Powerful forces were stirring which would soon show classical antiquity in a more inspiring light, and which would flower in the romantic Hellenism of the nineteenth century.

## Nineteenth Century

The explosive, romantic poets of the nineteenth century, with their intense subjectivity, found little satisfaction in or use for the objective epic phase of the Trojan legend. The greater aspirations and higher flights of the century found better expression in other ancient legends than that of Troy. But the wide assortment of minds and the diversity of conflicting philosophies crowded into the century assured to the Trojan legend, if not a dominant place in the thought, at any rate a minor place in the fancies and aspirations of the time. A marked trait of the century was its reverence for everything Greek, with the consequent disparagement of Latin culture, especially in its pinched, neoclassic form of the previous century. The Hellenism of the nineteenth century was in certain respects a fuller expression of that of Greece. Sentiment, idealism, melancholy, nature, the religious and philosophical temper, morality, mediaeval chivalry and romance, humor and realism all had fuller living room. Among the English poets there was no conflict between Hellenism and Romance. Romance lent to Hellenism a fuller realization of itself.

WORDSWORTH.—Wordsworth's *Laodamia,* coming out of his renewed interest in classical mythology and authors as sources for philosophical interpretations, gave the poet a mythological framework through which he expressed divinely the transcendence of self-sacrificing devotion over physical suffering and the reality of the unseen, intangible communion of the spirit with the Divine. An idealist and a contemplative poet with respect to the experience of living, Wordsworth teaches his age anew a code of behavior which minimizes the humiliation of dying. Laodamia gained a short reprieve from death for her husband Protesilaus, who met his death as the first of the Greeks to set foot upon Trojan soil, and then she died as he was taken from her. Much of the Trojan legend had become by this time common property and a permanent part of man's experience. It is idle to search too closely for specific sources. More important than the source is the new thought or interpretation embodied in the new telling of the story. But Wordsworth's chief indebtedness in this poem is to the sixth book of Vergil's *Aeneid.*[66]

LANDOR.—Landor's ventures in the Trojan legend lie in his *Achilles and Helena on Ida* and, from the *Hellenics:* the *Menelaus and Helen at Troy,* which opens with Menelaus in a rage of fury determined to slay Helen and closes with a reconciliation and rebirth of their early love; *The Espousals of Polyxena* and *The Death of Paris and Oenone.* In *The Espousals of Polyxena* that heroine is reconciled to wedlock with the living Achilles instead of, as in the ancient tradition, being sacrificed to the dead Achilles at his tomb. This romantic association of Polyxena with Achilles may be traced back through Caxton and Lydgate to Dictys. But in the temple at the wedding ceremony an arrow from a hostile hand finds its way to the vulnerable heel of Achilles, and when we leave him there is a farewell to his son Pyrrhus on his lips. Thus emotional tone and pathos are gained through both romance and death, the poet's way of accentuating the significance of life by associating it with the two experiences which make us aware of its passing. To the chafing, troubled seas of youthful heroes and heroines Landor often devotes himself. It seems best to consider Landor's story of Paris and Oenone in its proper place in the history of this story in literature.

PARIS AND OENONE FROM OVID TO TENNYSON.—The story of Paris and Oenone has been of perennial interest to poets. In its complete form it brings Paris, broken in pride and about to die from a wound dealt by Philoctetes, back to his first love Oenone, whom he had deserted, and who alone can heal him—a situation complicated by mingled feelings (among them a still lingering love of Oenone for Paris) and by the continued love of Paris for Helen. From the time of Homer, Paris seldom subjected himself to the vexation of thinking of the implications and consequences of his deeds, but in a poignant situation of this kind he must have tasted of the ashes of sin. Ovid's imaginary epistle of Oenone to Paris in his *Heroides* does not rise above his general Alexandrine level, where his sources lie. The pastoral setting is pretty, and toward the end of her epistle Oenone becomes sincere and affecting. But in Oenone's reference to her skill in the use of healing drugs there is no hint of her decision to abandon Paris to his fate and then to destroy herself. The story is also found in antiquity in the mythological handbook attributed to Apollodorus.

Here Oenone, refusing to heal Paris at first and then repenting too late, hung herself when she found him dead.[67] According to the version of Quintus of Smyrna, Paris, coming to Oenone against his will, blamed his betrayal of her on Fate and begged her help. With mockery and taunts she drove him back to Helen, though later in repentance she threw herself on his funeral pyre and died.

In Tennyson's early mythological idyl, *Oenone,* the betrayed wife of Paris laments on the hillside once blest by their love the award of the golden apple which took her lover from her. In Landor's poem, mentioned above, from which we approached this topic, Paris, carried to Oenone in a helpless condition, asks for pardon but not for help. Oenone seems to have been unnerved by an internal struggle, for she has none of that capacity for scorn and invective which she manifested in Quintus' version. Feeling that now at last Paris is her very own, she falls upon him with a request for a last embrace and a wish to die before him. Landor is neoclassic in spirit and another Ovid in emotional range. Being a man without anything distinctive to say he made fewer changes in his classical sources than any of his contemporaries. He can retell a story more easily than he can re-create one. Of himself he says that he was more diaphanous than prismatic. William Morris wrote *The Death of Paris,* a part of *The Earthly Paradise.* He invests his heroine with the perplexity of both pity and scorn, love and hatred. But the bitterness caused by Paris' betrayal of her was finally overcome by her female instinct for pity and love, and she began to relieve her former husband. Upon discovering, however, that Paris' heart still belonged to Helen, she withdrew her aid. Before departing she kissed him. Paris died alone, with the name of Helen on his lips. At the end of his life and sixty years after his early idyl on Oenone, Tennyson wrote *The Death of Oenone.* After Ibsen this heroine could hardly be expected to maintain the namby-pamby tradition of Landor and Morris regarding her. She is now free to assert herself with vigor. But at the end of the poem Oenone in a moment of rededication leaped upon the funeral pyre of Paris and perished, just as she had done in Tennyson's source, Quintus. Tennyson's poem, however, is not and was not intended to be a mere retelling of an ancient story. It bears within itself the genuine, if inorganic, preachment so dear to Tennyson regarding the ethical basis of England's glory and of human behavior, and Victorian England's social moralities.

ARNOLD.—Matthew Arnold in his *Palladium* leads one from the Palladium, for which as the symbol of Troy's continuance Hector fought in the plains below, to the human soul for which other Hectors and Ajaxes carry on, either to *rust in shade or shine in strife*. He moralizes as follows:

> Still doth the soul, from its lone fastness high,
> Upon our life a ruling effluence send.
> And when it fails, fight as we will, we die;
> And while it lasts, we cannot wholly end.

In this poem we see Arnold's true self. An ardent Hellenist, he found in mythology distilled of its dross through his purifying imagination a stabilizing force against the static and confusion of the contemporary.

MORRIS, ROSSETTI.—William Morris left unfinished and unpublished at his death his *Scenes from the Fall of Troy*, a curious revival of the mediaeval version of the story handed down from Dictys through the Middle Ages and into the Renaissance. The old characters of the Trojan War, clothed in mediaeval garb, speak thoughts that are neither ancient nor mediaeval. For Morris has infused into his characters his own brooding sense of the fleeting joy of living and of the futility of things. His characters accompany his inner self in an escape into a romanticized and idealized world of his own creation.

Rossetti's work on the Trojan legend lies in his pretty ballad *Troy Town* presenting Helen immune to a sense of guilt and in the flush of her sensual pagan beauty as she offers to Venus a cup molded from her breast; and in his sonnet *Death's Songsters,* in which Helen would have lured the Greeks within the wooden horse to their doom, had not Odysseus restrained them into silence.[68]

LANG, WILDE.—Andrew Lang has left a poem *Helen of Troy* (1882), a pretty re-creation of an innocent, simple Helen by a romantic sentimentalist living in an age in which Homeric naiveté and simplicity could be only a fictitious phantasy of the mind. His story begins with the coming of Paris to the home of Menelaus and ends with the translation of Helen and Menelaus to Elysium after their reconciliation is brought about by Aphrodite and after their many years of happy life together at home. Aphrodite instructs Helen in the policy which she must follow in her relations with Paris, and promises to make her oblivious of all the shame involved. Homer did not dwarf the initiative of his characters or whitewash them in this way. Even in Homer, where inner psychological forces are not expected to any great degree, Helen is an interesting character of some depth. She is made to rebel against her lot, though she must regretfully acquiesce in it; and she has a sense of the shame of her situation and of the reactions which that situation arouses in those who suffer for her.[69] To return to Lang's poem, the Trojan women made a social outcast of Helen. Paris unwittingly slew his son by Oenone, which drew the curse of Oenone upon him. With the coming of the Greek forces to Troy events move rapidly toward the destruction of the city. The poem closes with Lang's tribute, romantic and melancholy, to the eternal tradition of Helen, as follows:

O'er Helen's shrine the grass is growing green,
In desolate Therapnae; none the less
Her sweet face now unworshipp'd and unseen
Abides the symbol of all loveliness,
Of Beauty ever stainless in the stress
Of warring lusts and fears;—and still divine,
Still ready with immortal peace to bless
Them that with pure hearts worship at her shrine.[70]

Thus, true to itself the nineteenth century walks with its feet in the clouds and its head in the stars, in contrast with our own, which seems, too often, to have its feet in the sewer and its head up in the gutter. The millinery of Homer looms large in this poem of Lang, and for the post-Homeric part of his story he has borrowed much from Quintus of Smyrna, but his chief indebtedness was to William Morris. In his prose work *Adventures Among Books* Lang has devoted a chapter, *Paris and Helen,* to a review of the story of the two lovers, largely as told by Greek authors of the ancient world.

Oscar Wilde in his poem *The New Helen* finds refuge, from a life of despair, frustration, and resignation in which even the planets are tired, in a mystic, transcendentalized Helen incarnate with spiritual love.

Lily of love, pure and inviolate!
Tower of ivory! red rose of fire!

In Wilde, sentimental romanticism, cut off from its roots in life, bows its weary head and languishes away like one of Vergil's poppies in a rainstorm.

## TWENTIETH CENTURY

Surviving into the twentieth century the Trojan legend has taken on some of that century's varying moods and experiences. When despair, cynicism, and disillusionment stalk

79

abroad, it absorbs them. Nor can our legend escape reinterpretation in terms of the sociological experiences of our day. Poets, who live in an estate of their own, may prefer, either despite or because of the dominant mood of their time, the romantic idealism which became a part of the legend in the nineteenth century. And in the hands of the modern novelist the legend takes on the conceits and mannerisms of the contemporary period. At all events, it has continued to be used as a vehicle for the literary expression of contemporary and yet often of eternal interests.

BOTTOMLEY, BROOKE, CHAPMAN, AND OTHERS.—Gordon Bottomley's *The Last of Helen* (1902) is a Helen to end Helens. The poem portrays, not without a touch of cynicism, a disconsolate queen longing for the conquests of olden days and dragging on a contemptuous life of emptiness and neglect in Sparta. There are also Laurence Binyon's one-act tragedy, *Paris and Helen* (1906), Sara Teasdale's *Helen of Troy,* John Jay Chapman's *Homeric Scenes,* and Rupert Brooke's two sonnets called *Menelaus and Helen,* in the second of which

> ... Helen bears
> Child on legitimate child, becomes a scold,
> Haggard with virtue. Menelaus bold
> Waxed garrulous, and sacked a hundred Troys
> 'Twixt noon and supper.

James Flecker acknowledges the immortality of Helen in his *Destroyer of Ships, Men, Cities.* In Sara Teasdale's poem just mentioned Helen against the red wings of flame soaring above the city of Troy laments her destiny, blaming the gods and her parents for it. She speculates on the presence of sublimating love in the Elysian fields, and predicts for herself the immortality of being reborn always on the lips and in the hearts of men, and as Menelaus stands helpless before her

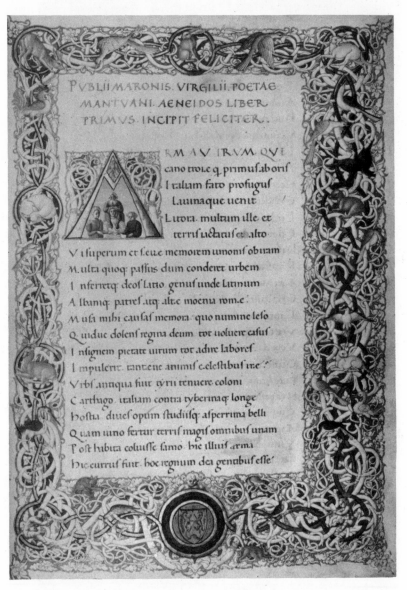

Vergil, codex 39-7, 1 recto.
Laurentian Library, Florence. See page 106

The "Paris-Master." *The Judgment of Paris.*

Courtesy of the Fogg Museum of Art, Cambridge, Massachusetts. See page 110

charm, foretells her return to conquer Greece again. Chapman's *Homeric Scenes* consists of two dramatizations called *Hector's Farewell,* enacted on the walls of Troy, and *The Wrath of Achilles,* divided into six different scenes. In the last scene Thetis, standing beside the tomb of Achilles, whom she tenderly and pathetically calls her wedding gift, says:

> Ah, my child,
> Thy short life leaves a glory in the world;
> And sea-born Thetis comes to guard thy tomb
> Beside the smiting music of the ocean,
> Where thou didst pace the sands and call on her
> In the great days of Troy.

Then there is E. L. Masters' *Helen of Troy,*[71] a pretty tribute to the direct appeal of Helen to the imagination of man and to the liberating quality by which her story sets free his fancies. Helen survived the first World War as well as that of which she was the direct cause. W. J. Turner has written a lyric *Paris and Helen* (1921).

MASEFIELD, BENÉT.—Masefield has used the legend of Troy in his tragedy in verse, *A King's Daughter* (1923), in his dramatic romance in prose, *The Taking of Helen* (1923), and in his *A Tale of Troy* (1932) in verse. To the base of an inherited tradition the poet has added his own fiction and the sociological interpretations natural to his time. If the dead of the Trojan War

> had forgotten
> The mud and death,
> The heat and flies
> Of the plain of Troy

and had forgiven Helen in whose cause the war was fought, they were little different from the generation of the twenties, which also tried hard to forget its recent war and to forgive. In an age fully aware of the sociological problems existing within itself, the Helen of the twenties—a pitiful, melancholy, pensive figure—bears her long overdue cross of suffering. But she found sympathy and comfort on every side and finally with her new husband sailed away, young and strong and peaceful, to rule forever in a land . . . where the sun is bright and skylarks never cease.[72] The quickening tempo of the world as it moved from the twenties to the thirties may be seen in the poet's condensation of a ninety-page account of the abduction of Helen into the following single stanza:

> So it was planned, so it was done,
> Paris and she were there at one,
> The sentry bribed and the door undone,
> With a waiting ship and a rising wind
> Helen was off with Priam's son.

But Masefield used a Homeric scene with high seriousness to express his hope for more enlightened times when Prime Minister Chamberlain flew to Berchtesgaden for a conference with the Nazi Chancellor prior to the outbreak of the second World War. His quatrain runs as follows:

> As Priam to Achilles for his son,
> So you into the night, divinely led,
> To ask that young men's bodies, not yet dead,
> Be given from the battle not begun.

Stephen Vincent Benét in *The Last Vision of Helen*[73] relates in ballad form the familiar story of the cause of the Trojan War, its consequences, and the flight of Helen's spirit to the Sphinx in Egypt. Helen, described as the alluring creation of the scarf of a cloud, desire and despair quickened into life by Zeus, blends with the Sphinx. The poem is cast in the form of a series of songs: of the City of Troy, the Sphinx, the men of Helen, and Helen. The theme is old, but the imagery, the music, and the vision are the new burden—and the new glory—which the story carries.

ERSKINE, MORLEY.—John Erskine's *The Private Life of Helen of Troy* brought to the American reader of light chitchat a realistically portrayed and completely modernized (for that time) Helen fully clothed with the trappings and the *mores* of contemporary life. In fact this book is said to have been one of the main factors which broke down the old code wherein the heroine must be young, beautiful, virtuous, and domestic, and brought in its place a flood tide of novels of license of which Margaret Mitchell's *Gone with the Wind* stands as a superb example, and in which life begins after and usually outside of marriage; nor need the heroine be beautiful provided she has personality; and seldom has she any high regard for virtue; nor does she know of or often go into the kitchen except to mix highballs.[74] To the same period belongs Edward Lucas White's romantic novel *Helen.* A worthy successor of Erskine's venture into the field of modernized legend in fiction is Christopher Morley's *The Trojan Horse* (1937). Starting with the external detail of characters and scene Morley has redressed his story with the furnishings of modern times and has psychologically adapted it to the modern point of view. The love of Troilus and Cressida needs to be reinterpreted to every age in terms of its contemporary *mores.* Aside from that, the distinctive flavor of the book lies in the projection of the keen, penetrating mind of Morley into his story, and in the incongruous burlesque of once exalted characters. Against a background of neon signs, skyscrapers, gas masks, stock market fluctuations, dinner parties, night club revues done by the Bosphorettes, cigarets and taxicabs, monacles and tuxedos, economic trends that apparently were as poorly understood but as loudly touted then as now, radio flashes, political radicalism and Toryism, patter-talk and badinage, smallness in evening dress and nobility in common garb, the twentieth century interpreted once more in terms of its own conceits and enthusiasms a time-honored story. As Morley philosophically points out, the blending of Now and Then makes Always.

# IV. THE LEGEND IN PAINTING CERAMICS, AND TAPESTRY

THE flowering through the centuries of the Trojan legend in the kindred pictorial arts of painting, ceramics, and tapestry is a major venture, figuratively speaking, in the field of mythological botany. The diversity of the blooms may be traced to the diversity of the subsoils out of which they have come. The general intellectual climate of any age, of course, affects the arts of that age. And one art in any age cannot be considered apart from the others in that age, and particularly apart from its own contemporary literature, for literature is the least perishable and most pervasive expression always of the cultural tradition. The remarkable thing about the story of Troy told in any art is not its fixity, but its adaptability; not that it is simply an old tale retold, but that it is new; that through that old tale workers in paint, clay, and wool mastered their respective trades and exalted them until they became fine arts; and that to pagan and Christian, to ancient and modern, to Greek, Roman, Italian, Englishman, Frenchman, German, to mention only a few, the tale gave an ennobling pride in humanity and a sense of humanity's dignity as it found expression in any of the fine arts.

## ANCIENT PAINTING

The creative force of the Trojan legend upon the mind and hand of the ancient painter might well be presumed, but Vitruvius, the author of a work on architecture who lived in the time of Augustus, assures us of the popularity of the Trojan War as a theme for painters.[1] It may be remembered that the atrium of Trimalchio's house in Petronius' bizarre *Trimalchio's Dinner* was adorned with pictures of the *Iliad* and the *Odyssey* and of a gladiatorial exhibition of Laenas![2] While painting offers to the artist a better medium of expression for the delineation of mythology than some of the other arts, yet painting is unfortunately one of the least durable of the arts in terms of the hazards of time and chance. A visualization of the history of painting in antiquity must too often be dimly comprehended through literary allusions and through badly worn Roman imitations of Greek originals, the very existence of which is often remote and sometimes doubtful. Little need be said about those paintings which survive only in testimonials regarding them.

Among the early Greek painters whose works survive only in this manner, for instance, are two. Cleanthes of Corinth painted, at Olympia, the sack of Troy,[3] an indication of this early artist's keen realization of the dramatic and emotional possibilities inherent in the story; and Calliphon of Samos painted for the sanctuary of Artemis, at Ephesus, the battle of the Greeks in defense of their ships at Troy,[4] a battle vividly described by Homer in the fifteenth book of the *Iliad*.

POLYGNOTUS.—The celebrated painter Polygnotus, an Ionian of Thasos of the middle of the fifth century B.C., employed the Trojan legend as his theme both at Delphi and Athens. For the clubroom of the Cnidians at Delphi, Polygnotus executed an elaborate ensemble of murals, life size or nearly so, on the sack of Troy and the departure of the Greeks. Pausanias[5] has left us in his valuable commentary that came out of his extensive travels in Greece in the second century of our era a minute description of these murals, a statement regarding their relative positions as he saw them, and suggestions as to possible literary sources for the paintings. It is worth observing in passing that these paintings were between five hundred and six hundred years old when Pausanias saw them. The three spheres of interest in this ensemble according to his description are as follows: Epeus tearing down the walls of Troy, Helen on the right, and Cassandra on the left.

It will be worth the trouble to note some details in Polygnotus' rendering of the story as thus reported to us. Helen sits on the shore, and above her sits Helenus in profound dejection. Andromache shares the miserable plight of the Trojan women; Astyanax clings to his mother. The tragic maiden, Polyxena, is also there on the strand. With Polygnotus is also to be associated the description of Polyxena, as found in the *Greek Anthology,* "in whose maidenly eyes lies the whole Trojan War."[6] Pausanias says that he had seen Polyxena's fate portrayed at both Athens and Pergamus. In another part of the group is Creusa, the wife of Aeneas. The tradition regarding her, according to Pausanias, was that the mother of the gods and Aphrodite saved her from slavery among the Greeks, because she was the wife of Aeneas. This tradition is retained by Vergil.[7] Epeus is demolishing the Trojan wall, and above the wall projects the head of his creation, the wooden horse. Ajax is there, and Cassandra sits on the ground with the image of Athena which she overturned when Ajax dragged her from sanctuary. Neoptolemus is the only Greek still on the rampage. He was so portrayed, says Pausanias, because this whole painting was to be put up over the grave of Neoptolemus, who was slain at Delphi. Being a man, Neoptolemus undoubtedly wanted to be remembered for manly deeds. Coroebus, the fiancé of Cassandra, lies dead, and so does Priam. As a sign to the Greeks to spare it in return for his previous hospitality to Menelaus and Odysseus, the house of Antenor is decorated with a leopard's skin. As already observed in a previous chapter, the posting of a leopard's skin on the house of Antenor and the escape of that Trojan hero himself, along with his family, were probably a part of the *Antenoridae* of Sophocles and, indeed, of even earlier works. Antenor himself, in the picture, stands close at hand with his family; all are in the throes of despair. The loading of an ass by his servants forecasts a journey ahead for him. Among the numerous attempts to reconstruct this work of Polygnotus on the basis of Pausanias' description, perhaps the most successful, is that of Robert.[8]

Polygnotus was familiar with the flourishing artistic work on the Trojan legend in sculpture, ceramics, and gem engraving, and he was a contemporary of Sophocles, Phidias, and Euripides, who all shared with him his interest in the Trojan legend. Also he inherited a rich literary tradition from the past, upon which he drew. Pausanias approached this ensemble of Polygnotus with a close familiarity with the entire epic tradition of the fall of Troy before his time. His observations regarding the paintings of Polygnotus and of the epic tradition make clear that Polygnotus used the epic tradition with independent judgment, that he followed no one author slavishly, and that he felt no hesitation in re-creating to suit his own artistic and esthetic purposes and adding to the tradition out of his own imagination. No fine distinction can be drawn in classical antiquity between Homer and the cyclic epics. Both were used for their dramatic action, and artists of ability, interested more in re-creation than in reproduction, could supply whatever they wished by way of interpretation of action. To be sure, Polygnotus' main literary source for his subject was the post-Homeric cyclic epic.

This great master of painting, one of a family of painters, who for his services accepted honor more willingly than money, expressed through his art that flush of national pride, that interest in idealism and in nobility of character which pervades the literature and other artistic forms of the generations after Marathon. To Aristotle and other ancient critics the greatest claim of Polygnotus' art lay in its ability to lift the soul of man above the commonplace. The artist seems to represent in painting, as did Sophocles in tragedy, not the heat and excitement of physical action, but the serene nobility and pathos of human beings suffering from the consequences of preceding crises in their lives. And so he avoids the carnage in the fall of Troy, as related by poets of the cyclic epic. Helen sits on the shore, instead of being forcibly led to the ships by Menelaus. Astyanax clings to his mother instead of being slain. The slaying of Polyxena and of Priam, too, is avoided by the painter, for Polyxena is still alive and Priam already dead. Ajax is represented at the altar instead of in the act of using violence against Cassandra. Only because of the peculiar association of the murals with Neoptolemus is that warrior allowed to run rampant.

Along with this interest in what we think of as classical serenity, which Polygnotus shares with the best artists of his day, he achieved a new technical skill. With him painting ceased to consist of lines drawn on a surface and then filled in with color. His paintings had depth, life, and expression.

In the Painted Porch in the market place at Athens, Polygnotus also painted a scene depicting the Greek chieftains in assembly deliberating on the violation of Cassandra by Ajax. Included in the picture were Ajax, Cassandra, and other captive women.[9]

Still visible to Pausanias in the late second century were some paintings in the picture gallery of the Propylaea at Athens. The two of these which dealt directly with Troy portrayed Odysseus taking the image of Athena, and Polyxena about to be slain near the tomb of Achilles. Whether Polygnotus should be given credit for painting these two works cannot be determined exactly from the words of Pausanias, who gives us our information about them.[10]

OTHER PAINTERS.—Panaenus and his celebrated brother, the sculptor Phidias, worked on a set of paintings to adorn the throne in the great temple of Zeus at Olympia. The scenes were mythological. Among them were the death of Penthesilea at the hands of Achilles, and the outrage of Ajax upon Cassandra.[11]

The famous painter Zeuxis, of the late fifth century, won considerable renown for his painting of Helen, which he made for the temple of Lacinian Juno at Croton in southern Italy, as a synthesis of five nude models whom the people of Croton supplied for him.[12]

It is evident from a survey of all available source material that Helen was a favorite subject for the painters, as were also Priam, Achilles, Agamemnon, and Menelaus.

Parrhasius, of the fourth century, painted the story of Ajax and Odysseus contending for Achilles' armor, in unsuccessful competition with Timanthes, who painted the same theme.[13]

The portrayal of myths in sequences of pictures and in sculptural blocks is known from Hellenistic times. As an example, a painter Theoros made a sequence on the Trojan War in the Porticus Philippi at Rome in the third century B.C. The story of the madness of Ajax, deranged by his loss of the arms of Achilles to Odysseus, and his slaughter of the cattle at Troy during his derangement was painted by Timomachus. Julius Caesar is said to have paid a large sum of money for this painting.[14] The cycle of paintings in the temple of Juno at Carthage, which Aeneas was supposed to have seen, portrayed the war around Troy and the events leading up to the fall of the city. Vergil is believed to be referring in his text to actual works of art known to his day. Finally, the life of

# PAINTING, CERAMICS, AND TAPESTRY

Achilles was the theme of a number of sequences in painting and sculpture from classical to mediaeval times.

INFLUENCE ON MOSAICS AND METAL ENGRAVING.—The arts of both painting and sculpture in the ancient world also exercised influence upon the selection of subjects used by the makers of mosaics and by the engravers of metal objects.

A mosaic of the fifth century B.C., found by Dr. David M. Robinson at Olynthus in 1934, represents Thetis and the Nereids bringing a shield, spear, and helmet to the seated Achilles. The mosaic is a composite of two passages of the eighteenth book of the *Iliad*, one at its beginning and the other at its end. One of the finest mosaics of the Hellenic period, it is done in white, black, red, green, and yellow pebbles. The names of Thetis and Achilles are inscribed on the mosaic. The mosaic is more than ten feet long and more than three feet wide.

Hieron II of Syracuse had a ship made under the super-intendence of Archimedes, the cabins of which had mosaic floors depicting the entire story of the *Iliad*. These stories were also inlaid in the furniture, ceilings, and doors.[15]

Scenes from the Trojan legend on Etruscan mirrors also testify to its popularity among Etruscan artists. Over a score of surviving Etruscan mirrors bear the story of the judgment of Paris. Other designs on Etruscan mirrors are the Trojan horse, and Agamemnon as he receives the Palladium from Diomedes. A fine engraved Etruscan mirror in the Metropolitan Museum, a work of the fourth century B.C., shows Aphrodite persuading Helen to join Paris. An Etruscan mirror in the British Museum in London portrays Helen in her boudoir with three female attendants and Aphrodite.[16]

Also, two Roman silver jugs of the time of Claudius found at Bernay in France over a century ago serve as a symbol of a highly specialized skill which had a long tradition in classical Greece and Italy. These two jugs are engraved with six scenes from the Trojan legend: the grief of Achilles over the corpse of his friend, Patroclus, the ransoming of Hector, the defilement of Hector's body before the walls of Troy and in sight of his parents, the death of Achilles, the meeting of Diomedes and Odysseus with Dolon, and the theft of the Palladium. The engraving of epic themes on metal objects was widespread in classical antiquity.[17]

EXTANT PAINTINGS.—A few paintings of scenes from the Trojan legend have survived from the ancient world. These paintings, turning up in separated places, suggest that there was a considerable traffic of patterns, legends, and probably even of artists, flowing from Greece to the Etruscans. (This movement is also evident in the gems, metalwork, and vases.)

One of the earliest representations of Greek mythology in painting comes out of Etruscan Italy and belongs to the first half of the sixth century B.C. In the Tomb of the Bulls at Corneto has been found a mural depicting Achilles surprising the youthful Troilus as the latter rode on horse to a fountain.[18] (With contemporary vase painters, too, this was a popular subject, as will be seen later.)

The François tomb, discovered at Vulci in 1857, reveals some paintings belonging to the end of the fourth century. Among them were scenes from the Trojan War, such as the insult of Ajax to Cassandra and the slaughter of Trojan captives by Achilles as an expiatory offering to Patroclus.[19]

Upon a sarcophagus found at Orvieto are some painted reliefs of the Trojan legend depicting the sacrifice of Polyxena at the tomb of Achilles and of Trojans at the tomb of Patroclus.[20] This sarcophagus is dated around the year 300 B.C.

A wall painting found at Herculaneum caricatures the flight of Aeneas with his father and son by depicting all three figures with the heads of dogs or baboons.

Several of the Pompeian murals have to do with the Trojan

legend. One depicts Paris on Mt. Ida.[21] The judgment of Paris was a favorite subject among the artists of Pompeii. Another mural represents on a large scale the surrender of Briseis by Achilles. The delineation of character in the faces of Achilles, Patroclus, and Briseis, the variety of colors in the various costumes, and the skillful composition of foreground and background make this a worthy re-creation of a memorable scene of the *Iliad*.[22] It seems agreed that this painting of the surrender of Briseis goes back to a Greek original of the fourth century, but it is idle to carry speculation on the subject further. Other frescoes of Pompeii depict Paris and Helen;[23] Neptune and Apollo building the walls of Troy; Aeneas wounded; Achilles playing the lyre; Ares and Aphrodite; Hephaestus forging the arms of Achilles in the presence of Thetis (a common theme); Thetis bringing to Achilles his new armor; the defilement of Hector's corpse before the walls of Troy and the ransoming of it; the introduction of the wooden horse into Troy by moonlight;[24] and the theft of the Palladium from Troy.[25] The painting of the introduction of the wooden horse into Troy by moonlight bears a close resemblance to the verses of Vergil. The horse enters from the left through a breach in the wall. It is pulled along by Trojan men and women, as children dance before it and worshipers with sacred branches and women with torches accompany it in procession to the temple of Athena. Before a statue of Athena, in front of her shrine, a kneeling woman, probably Cassandra, prays with outstretched hands. An aged man seated near by in despair must represent Priam. On a hill above this scene a woman, doubtless Helen, waves a torch high in the air, thereby, as in Vergil, signaling to the Greeks to return under cover of night:

> *Flammam media ipsa tenebat*
> *ingentem, et summa Danaos ex arce vocabat.*[26]

93

Finally, two paintings in the Golden House of Nero in Rome portrayed the famous parting of Hector and Andromache before the walls of Troy and the story of Paris and Helen.

In the former of the two paintings Hector clad in golden helmet, blue chiton, breastplate, and greaves, stands before the city wall with a nurse and maidservant, and Andromache, who holds her son in her arms.[27]

## GREEK CERAMICS

HISTORY.—An older sister of Greek painting was the ceramic art, which also gave expression to the legend. The story of the legend of Troy on Greek vases, however, should be read against a background of the general history of Greek ceramics, its limitations, peculiar successes, and literary sources of inspiration. The Greeks in general, and in particular the Athenians, raised to a fine art the manufacture and adornment of vases. Appropriately enough, the Greek word for potter's clay has become our word "ceramic." Greek vases are of two kinds, black figured and red figured. The black-figured style, that of silhouette and incision, came to Athens at the end of the seventh century B.C. Steady progress ensued in the refining of the shapes of vases and in the drawing and variety of the figures.

Attic pottery was exported far and wide as early as 625-600 B.C. Shortly after 600 B.C. Attic vases made their appearance in Egypt, southern Russia, and Etruria, providing eloquent testimony of the rising commercial and artistic ascendance of Athens. By the middle of the sixth century the Attic vase had established its supremacy over all rivals, and was to keep it, practically unchallenged, for a century. The increasing use of signatures indicates the artists' pride in workmanship.

About the year 525 B.C. the custom came in, and from that time on held the field, of leaving the inscribed figures of the vase in the red color of the clay and painting the background black. Then shortly after the introduction of this "red-figured" technique the vase painters acquired the ability to lend to their figures on the vases an illusion of depth, solidity, and roundness, a skill which sculpture of that time still reveals.

A growing social consciousness in Athens also manifested itself on Attic vases in a new dignity and reserve in the figures.

Then, too, the progress made by Polygnotus in painting with expression and characterization imparted a considerable stimulus to the vase painters, who, however, were unable to reproduce in their pottery the significant contributions which Polygnotus made to murals. In general the vase painter mastered his trade more quickly than other contemporary artists did theirs. But it should also be said that the capacities of vase painting, even at their full, are lower than those of the major Greek arts, which, though they came to full fruition later, yet were more capable of carrying the message of mature Athens than was the vase painter with his miniature art. And at the time of the full tide of the Athenian achievement the painter of vases had become just a craftsman in a city of artists. One does not, however, expect the same depth in tone of a harp as of an organ, so perhaps no comparison of the art media should be suggested.

The vase paintings of the sixties and fifties in the fifth century B.C. have in general lost the freshness, vitality, and vigor of their predecessors. In the fourth century the art went into a complete decline.

But even with the inherent limitations of the medium of ceramics, the Greek artist at his best expressed through his clay and paint the message which his fellow artists were to express through marble and words. It is the Greek message of a "dream of form in days of thought," to use Austin Dobson's phrase, of esthetic beauty achieved through proportion, design, and harmony, and of undisturbed and unsuspecting charm, simplicity, and delicate grace.

In contrast with the vast literature which has grown up in modern times around the subject of Greek ceramics, such was the reticence of the Greek about his work that the entire business of vase painting is mentioned just once in ancient Greek literature, and most of the extant Greek vases, even the best ones, are unsigned.

EPIC TRADITION.—The artist's message was expressed through the design of the vase itself and also through the lively scenes, drawn usually from daily life and mythology, which adorned the vase. Scenes from mythology recur on Greek vases with the same regularity and were inspired by the same sense of sympathetic devotion as were the Annunciations in the Renaissance. Though the vase painters, along with other contemporary artists, must have been profoundly affected by Homer, yet they drew broadly from the epic tradition as a whole, not restricting themselves to Homer and seldom following any literary tradition with close fidelity. In the very nature of the case it is not entirely satisfactory to re-create Homer on a Greek vase, any more than it would be to play Beethoven's *Moonlight Sonata* on a lute. But within the given limitations of his art the vase painter created a fine art out of a trade. The following pages will show the extent to which the Greek vase painters used the legend of Troy.

### Scenes Prior to Opening of the Iliad

A very popular subject among the Greek vase painters of antiquity was the judgment of Paris, a part of the lost epic *Cypria*, the stories of which seem to have been preferred to those of the *Iliad* by Greek vase painters. The examples of this famous story surviving on Greek vases are sufficient to reveal a rather distinct historical development of the story.[28]

Rubens. *The Judgment of Paris.* National Gallery, London. See page 112

Gozzoli. *The Abduction of Helen*. National Gallery, London. See page 113

# PAINTING, CERAMICS, AND TAPESTRY

In one type of presentation Paris does not appear at all before the procession of goddesses led by Hermes; in another group of vases only reluctantly and even with a show of resistance to Hermes does he consent to render judgment on so delicate a matter. In time, however, he assumes his task in stride and with composure.

No distinct crystallization of the story or conformity with any literary tradition becomes evident in a study of the many extant versions of the story on vases, but a charm, grace, and individualism will be found in the interpretation and adornment of the story by the great masters of the period after the Persian War.

The award of the golden apple which Eris, the goddess of Strife, introduced as a disturbing element into the wedding of Peleus and Thetis in revenge for not having been invited is not commonly found in the literary sources until the Roman Empire. Although the presence of Eris at the wedding banquet, the contest among the three goddesses, and the judgment of Paris were, according to Proclus, all a part of the cyclic epic *Cypria,* yet the author does not specifically mention the golden apple as a factor in the rivalry. There are references to the apple in the scholia of Euripides, in Servius' commentary on the *Aeneid* (where it is specifically called "golden"), and in Lucian. Yet its recurrence on Etruscan mirrors leaves little doubt of the knowledge of this phase of the legend in the heyday of Greek art. On some Etruscan vases, however, the object held by Paris is definitely oval and has been regarded as either a pear or an egg, with some symbolic Orphic or Bacchic meaning.

There is a fine portrayal of the judgment of Paris on a red-figured *cylix* (drinking cup) bearing the signature of the famous potter Hieron.[29] Paris, surrounded by his flock, sits with his lyre. Hermes approaches, and behind him come Athena,

Hera, and Aphrodite, attended by four flying *Erotes* or Cupids. The painter of this *cylix,* considered to be Macron, attained a marked beauty in his portrayal of female dress. This cup is considered one of his best pieces. On it there is also a portrayal of the abduction of Helen by Paris.[30]

The finest white *pyxis* (covered jar) in existence, in the Metropolitan Museum in New York, painted in black, brown, and purple and dated in the first half of the fifth century B.C., also portrays the judgment of Paris. Here again Hermes, attended by the three goddesses, approaches the seated Paris.[31] The small Cupids found on Hieron's *cylix* do not recur here, but a boy with large wings enters into the composition. The painting of this particular jar is attributed to the "Penthesilea painter." The white *pyxis* had a brief vogue in this late archaic period. In Berlin a red-figured jar of the same period bears the same scene. Many other interpretations of this same story may be found on vases, including an early *hydria* and two *amphoras* in London, a *stamnos* (large jar) in Berlin, and *hydrias* in Naples and Carlsruhe.

TROILUS.—The tragic story of Priam's young son, Troilus, was also a favorite with the Greek vase painters. A recurring scene on black-figured vases is that of Achilles crouching behind a tree as he waits for Troilus to come to a spring.

That queen of vases, the François vase at Florence, bears four scenes portraying the ambush and slaying of Troilus, as follows: his approach to a fountain outside the city wall to water his horses in company with his sister Polyxena; the pursuit of him by Achilles; the announcement of his death to Priam; and the departure of Hector and Polites for rescue or revenge. This vase is a black-figured *crater* (mixing bowl) of the archaic period, found at Chiusi, and is one of the most celebrated Greek vases in existence by virtue of its form and of the variety, expressiveness, and elegance of its figures. It bears the signatures of the potter, Ergotimus, and of the painter, Clitias,[32] artists who established the supremacy of the Attic vase even in Etruria.

A black-figured *hydria* (water jar) in the Boston Museum of Fine Arts bears on its shoulder a portrayal of the pursuit of Troilus by Achilles. Fully armed, Achilles pursues Troilus, who rides one of a pair of horses and brandishes his whip as he looks back. His sister Polyxena runs ahead of the horses. She has dropped the water jar which on the left of this scene she is represented as filling.

The scene of Achilles slaying Troilus at an altar is found on red-figured vases, too.

### Scenes from the Iliad

Most of the famous scenes of the *Iliad* may be found on Greek vases. Some of these scenes may be listed as follows: the quarrel of Agamemnon and Achilles and the consequent seizure of Briseis; Thersites insulting Agamemnon; the duel between Menelaus and Paris; the wounding of Aeneas by Diomedes and the rescue of him by his mother, Aphrodite;[33] the farewell of Hector to Andromache and Astyanax; the combat of Ajax and Hector; the embassy to Achilles; the capture of Dolon and the theft of the horses of Rhesus by Odysseus and Diomedes; the prowess of Aeneas; the battle at the Greek ships; Patroclus going to battle; the combat over the body of Patroclus; Achilles mourning for his dead friend; Thetis in the workshop of Hephaestus; the presentation of new armor to Achilles; Hector being pursued by Achilles around the walls of Troy; the death of Hector; the funeral of Patroclus and the games in honor of him; and Priam begging Achilles for the corpse of Hector.

A red-figured *cotyle* (two-handled cup) in the Louvre, bearing the signature of Hieron, portrays the seizure of Briseis by Agamemnon, who, contrary to the version of Homer, himself leads his captive maiden by the wrist into his tent. She is followed by his herald Talthybius and by Diomedes, who takes no part at all in the Homeric version of this story. Briseis modestly raises a veil to her face.[34] On the other side of this cup is portrayed the embassy of Ajax, Odysseus, and Phoenix to the tent of Achilles at the suggestion of the penitent Agamemnon, another recurring subject of Greek vase paintings. The painter of this cup is thought to be Macron.[35] A *cylix* in the Louvre painted by the well-known Athenian artist Duris carries the scene of the duel between Menelaus and Paris, which forms part of the third book of the *Iliad*. Menelaus with drawn sword lunges after Paris, who gives way in fright. The goddess, Artemis, who stands to the right of Paris, raises her hand in intervention. Aphrodite, standing behind Menelaus, checks his hand as he prepares to strike. The scene on this cup shows well the independence of the Homeric tradition exercised by the painter, for the two versions have in common only the flight of Paris. Paris, in fact, appears in a worse light on the vase than in Homer, for on the cup he retreats in full possession of his spear.[36] On the reverse of this cup is a spirited version of the combat of Ajax and Hector, which Homer relates in the seventh book of the *Iliad*.[37] Duris put into his work an ease and suppleness.

An early *calyx crater* in Boston, magnificent in size, shape, and general composition, bears two scenes from the Trojan War: on one side Diomedes, assisted by Athena, strikes down Aeneas, who is protected by Aphrodite; and on the other Achilles and Memnon with Athena and with Eos, who is Memnon's mother and goddess of the dawn, encourages them in their fight over the corpse of Melanippus.[38] There is Homeric vigor in the scenes.

A red-figured *lecythus* (flask) in the Metropolitan Museum

of Art in New York bears an unusually poignant representation of a scene described by Homer, vividly though differently: the grief of Achilles over the corpse of his dear friend, Patroclus. In his hut on the Trojan plain Achilles is represented as sitting motionless on a chair with both hands folded on his lap and with head bowed. The body of Patroclus lies beside him on a bier. Achilles' mother, Thetis, and her sister Nereids come riding across the sea on dolphins in response to his prayers, and bring the pieces of the armor made by Hephaestus. The Nereids are exquisitely dressed in belted chitons, mantles, necklaces, earrings, and bracelets, and they have fillets in their hair. Their names, inscribed on the vase, are among those as listed in those lovely lines of Homer and as reproduced in a version of Robert Bridges.[39] The entire scene of Achilles, Patroclus, and the Nereids occupies the middle zone of the vase and is executed in polychrome on a white ground. The vase is ascribed to the "Eretria painter."[40]

A red-figured *cylix* in the Boston Museum of Fine Arts has what is thought to be the best representation on extant vases of the death of Hector in the siege of Troy. It may well be studied with a text of Homer in hand. Achilles pursues Hector before the walls of Troy, while within the walls may be seen Athena, Priam, and Hecuba, the latter two in tears.[41]

A *lecythus,* in the Metropolitan Museum, has a representation in black figures of Achilles outraging the body of Hector. The charioteer of Achilles, clothed in white, drags Hector by the feet in a two-horse chariot. Achilles runs along beside the chariot. The ghost of Patroclus rises above his tomb, where the scene is laid. A serpent beneath the horses symbolizes death, and a tree, the Trojan plain.[42]

A red-figured *cotyle* in Vienna, attributed to the celebrated potter Brygos, bears a portrayal of the aged Priam, followed by attendants laden with gifts, entering the tent of Achilles to ransom his son, who lies prostrate with bound hands and wounded sides under the couch of Achilles. The helmet, shield, sword, and cloak of Achilles hang in the background.[43]

### Scenes Subsequent to the Iliad

The legends of the Trojan War beyond the close of the *Iliad* are also well represented on ancient vases. The fortunes of Achilles after the death of Hector made a strong appeal to the imaginations of the vase painters. The principal episodes in this section of the legend are Achilles' victories over Penthesilea and Memnon, his own death, and the tragic events coming out of the award of his armor. After a valiant career on the field of battle, Penthesilea, queen of the Amazons, was finally slain by Achilles, who then, moved by her beauty in death, slew Thersites for scoffing at him.

A very early red-figured *hydria* in the Metropolitan Museum attributed to the "Berlin painter," one of the two most gifted painters of large vases in his period, shows in careful and beautiful workmanship the victory of Achilles over Penthesilea. As Penthesilea falls back, mortally wounded, she extends her right hand for mercy. Blood flows from her wounds.

But the belated love which Achilles conceived for his fallen opponent is not as evident on this vase as on the late archaic *cylix* in Munich from which the "Penthesilea painter" gets his name. The interpretation of the death of Penthesilea on this *cylix* is thought to have been inspired by some great painting, perhaps a painting of Polygnotus. The "Penthesilea painter," whose masterpiece this is, was a great artist of the seventies and sixties in the fifth century. The story of Achilles' love for Penthesilea does not appear in extant classical literature until Roman times, though it seems that the *Aethiopis* of the Greek epic period had Achilles slay Thersites because Thersites had accused him of loving Penthesilea.[44]

# PAINTING, CERAMICS, AND TAPESTRY

A large red-figured *amphora* or possibly a *crater* (two-handled mixing bowl) in the Boston Museum of Fine Arts, made in Apulia in southern Italy in the fourth century B.C., portrays the fate of Thersites. Achilles is attended by Phoenix. In the foreground lies the headless body of Thersites, and a short distance away his head. Diomedes, Menelaus, and soldiers are also portrayed in vigorous action.[45]

The story of the sack of Troy, like that of Penthesilea, provided the vase painters of the ancient world along with men in every field of artistic expression with an abundant source of material packed with emotion. Extant vases preserve for us many illustrations of this part of the Trojan legend, as, for example, the theft of the Palladium by Odysseus and Diomedes; the story of the wooden horse; the death of Laocoön; the violent seizure of Cassandra by Ajax; the death of Priam and Astyanax; the recovery of Helen by Menelaus;[46] the flight of Aeneas; and the sacrifice of Polyxena.

Renderings of the sack of Troy around the middle of the fifth century are more common than they are inspired. The vase painter's attempt to compete with mural painting only serves to remind one of his growing limitations. A *cylix* in Munich depicts Epeus as he carves the Trojan horse with hammer and chisel in the presence of Athena and two old men. A red-figured vase in Berlin represents Athena as modeling a horse in clay. Readers of Vergil will remember that the wooden horse which brought about the downfall of Troy was made *divina Palladis arte*.[47] Athena is portrayed as working in the shop of Epeus, whose bow, drill, and saw hang on the wall behind her. She is engaged in finishing off the nose of the horse, which otherwise has been practically completed. Evidently the work of Athena will serve as a model for Epeus.[48] A fragment of a south-Italian *crater* in Milan portrays the abduction of the Palladium by Ajax. A priestess stands aghast with horror, and Cassandra lays a violent hand on the irreverent pillager.[49] A red-figured *column crater* in Rome has on it a version of the death of Priam,[50] and a late red-figured *volute crater* in Bologna associated with the "Niobid painter" portrays with shocking vividness the slaying of Priam by Neoptolemus. This violent warrior, having seized the aged king as, scepter in hand, he sits on the altar of Zeus, is pummeling him with the corpse of Astyanax, which he whirls through the air, holding it by one leg.[51] Another of the numerous representations of this theme is on a *lecythus* in the British School at Athens. As Priam is on the point of being slain, a woman, either Hecuba or Andromache, standing beside him lifts her left hand to her head in token of grief and her right hand in a gesture of supplication to the young warrior. Neoptolemus is apparently on the point of hurling the head of Astyanax into the face of Priam.

The interpretation on Greek vases of the death of Priam falls into three rather distinct categories: that in which Neoptolemus slays Priam alone at the altar, that in which Astyanax is being hurled by the leg at Priam, and that in which the head of Astyanax is hurled at Priam.[52]

A third scene subsequent to the *Iliad* used by ceramic artists is the flight of Aeneas.

A black-figured *cylix* of the late sixth century B.C. found at Vulci and bearing the signature of the Athenian potter Nicosthenes, carries on it a portrayal of Aeneas carrying Anchises on his back and accompanied by Ascanius.[53] The discovery of this *cylix* in Italy corroborates other evidence of a widespread knowledge of the legend of Aeneas and a natural interest in it, in the West among the early Etruscans before the time when we can think of anything distinctly Roman. By the middle of the sixth century B.C. Athenian artists dominated the Etrurian market. There is also a black-figured *oinochoë* (wine pitcher) attributed to Nicosthenes which portrays Aeneas carrying Anchises and followed by Creusa.[54]

Many other portrayals of the flight of Aeneas with his family from Troy have survived and show that it was a very common theme on black-figured vases.[55]

A white *lecythus* found in Sicily, though undoubtedly made in Athens, presents a unique rendering of the flight of Aeneas and his father from Troy. As Aeneas advances toward the right he looks back at his father, whom he is guiding. With his right hand he grasps Anchises by the right wrist, and in his left hand he bears a shield and a spear. He wears a short chiton, some kind of armored apron, a scarf over his shoulders, and a high Corinthian helmet. On the left, the blind Anchises follows his son, gropingly feeling his way along with a cane held in his left hand. Some traces of their names remain on the vase. There is an unusual pathos and psychological penetration in the difficulty with which the aged father proceeds under pressure and in the solicitude of Aeneas as he must perforce overtax the powers of his sire.[56]

Many other vase paintings bearing on the Trojan legend can be discovered readily by consulting the indices of the handbooks on Greek vases.[57]

### ILLUMINATED MANUSCRIPTS OF HOMER AND VERGIL

The art of illustrating and embellishing manuscripts enjoyed a long historical development in both Europe and the East through the centuries connecting the ancient and the modern world. Illuminated manuscripts of Homer and Vergil, forming part of the treasures of many famous libraries of Europe, lend continuity of the rôle of the Trojan legend in the cultural and artistic history of Europe.

In the Ambrosian Library at Milan is a fragmentary vellum manuscript of the *Iliad* embellished with colored drawings illustrating the poem and dating in the third or fourth century of our era.

In the Vatican Library are two illuminated manuscripts of Vergil belonging probably to the fourth century.

The opening of the *Aeneid* with very elegant embellishments of border, miniature, and initial letters may be seen on the first page of a very ornate vellum manuscript in the Laurentian Library at Florence, a work of the fifteenth century. The dimensions of the page are about nine by thirteen inches. The miniature in the upper left corner of the text depicts the wooden horse and the destruction of Troy. In the elaborate border surrounding the text on all four sides, amid a luxurious wealth of detail, are scenes familiar to readers of the *Aeneid*—such as the judgment of Paris, the departure of Aeneas from Dido, and his arrival in Italy.

Another elegant vellum manuscript of the works of Vergil, a manuscript of the fifteenth century, in the Laurentian Library at Florence, bearing the desk-number 39-7, is worthy of its fine tradition in the history of manuscript illumination. The size of its pages is slightly more than eight by twelve inches. The initials, the titles beginning the books, the miniatures, and the elaborate border adorning the first page of each of the works of Vergil in this manuscript are done in gold. The initial letters of each line are also in gold. The miniature on the page beginning the *Aeneid* (1 recto) portrays Aeneas with Ascanius, Creusa, and Anchises.

Another fine manuscript of Vergil in the Laurentian Library is that listed as Riccardiana 492. Among the many adornments of this beautiful manuscript are the miniatures which occupy the bottoms of many of its pages and are designed to illustrate the script above them. On the bottom of page 61 (verso) is a miniature depicting the judgment of Paris and the abduction of Ganymede by the eagle of Jupiter. And on page 80 (recto) of this same manuscript the miniature depicts the entrance of the wooden horse into Troy. These miniatures are about two and a half by five inches in size.

Other miniatures of Florentine codices of Vergil may be found reproduced in Schubring's work on *cassoni*. The miniatures are of course designed to illustrate the text of Vergil, though the interpretations are made in terms of contemporary dress and architectural background. They portray such subjects as the following: Laocoön with the serpents and the wooden horse; the Greek heroes emerging from the wooden horse under cover of night; Hector appearing to Aeneas in a dream; the struggle in the streets of Troy; the death of Androgeus; the death of Panthus; Pyrrhus gaining entrance to a window by a ladder; Priam putting on his armor; the death of Polites; the death of Priam; the appearance of Venus before Aeneas; Aeneas preparing for flight with his wife, child, and father with the miraculous sign from heaven above the head of Anchises; and the ghost of Creusa appearing to Aeneas amid the ruins of Troy.[58] These elegant manuscripts may be regarded as the outer symbols of the great humanistic revival in Italy, in which Vergil played a conspicuous rôle.

## PAINTING, CHIEFLY OF THE RENAISSANCE

RENAISSANCE AND CLASSICAL ART.—The great masters of the Renaissance had unremitting demands made upon their time by the Church for religious work and by their secular patrons for portraiture. But at the same time they came to classical mythology, especially as transmitted through Ovid, with a new freshness and found in this mythology an insistent appeal. Abundant renderings of the Trojan legend are found from this early period of revival. Sometimes the stories are charmingly reinterpreted in terms of the dress and life of the Italian Renaissance.

The Classics cannot be asked to survive in any other way than through reinterpretation; though, to be sure, merely to interpret an old story in the dress of one's own time does not of itself make the story contemporary, except in dress, or significant, any more than to interpret it in the dress of antiquity makes it necessarily obsolete or unimportant. As a matter of fact, the classical tradition was so imperfectly known to some ages that they had no choice except to see it in terms of their own dress. The Renaissance made considerable progress in comprehending classical antiquity, at least in its Roman phase, but its knowledge of those times was naturally less than obtained in the neoclassical revival of the eighteenth century. At all events, the dress of a mythological painting is not as important as the capacity of the artist to create through his art, regardless of dress, a total human experience or an authentic feeling. The Homeric poems themselves have the capacity to equate the classroom of a university with universality itself. Without them universality would be less universal.

In many Renaissance interpretations of the Trojan legend the artists have availed themselves of the growing acquaintance with classical antiquity. The prevalence of the nude in ancient sculpture led to an adoption of it by both sculptors and painters of the Renaissance, who in some cases were identical. Both anatomy and drapery received considerable study under the stimulus of ancient accomplishments in these fields. The enthusiasm of the Renaissance for classical antiquity led not merely to a superficial imitation of classical art, but to an attempted re-creation of the classical spirit. Both Ghiberti and Masaccio created draped and undraped figures. Donatello's David was made in the spirit and after a close study of Hellenistic art. In the later Renaissance, Pollaiuolo, Luca Signorelli, and Titian made further progress in their mastery of the nude in painting; Michelangelo used the nude figure in both painting and sculpture; but Andrea Mantegna had a marked capacity to re-create the ancient in its own dress. Raphael was also much interested in ancient sculpture.

But whatever the manner of interpretation, whether in dress, contemporary or ancient, or in the nude, yet in the realm of the spirit the Renaissance was able to bring to the legend of Troy an authentic freshness, a spontaneous enthusiasm, a vivacity, and a charm. These qualities are the capital of the Renaissance artist. With them his work remains contemporary even in later times when the costumes of his characters have passed out of vogue.

*Cassoni.* JUDGMENT OF PARIS AND OTHER THEMES.—An interesting chapter in the history of painting was worked out, during the early Renaissance, particularly in Florence and Siena, in the application of this art to the decoration of all kinds of domestic furniture and of ornamental articles (especially the chest or *cassone,* which was a part of the furniture of the Renaissance home). The word *cassone* has become a generic one used to denote any domestic article of an ornamental nature. The exhaustive treatise of Schubring on such articles has as its title this word in its plural form, *cassoni.* The development of this field of painting came through the well-known artists of the Italian Renaissance in Florence and Siena and their schools. In some paintings the artists can be identified, and in others their identity has to be conjectured (as in the case of Greek vases) through a study of stylistic traits. A study of these paintings will carry one into the careers and influence of such artists as Fra Angelico, Jacopo del Sellaio, Domenico Ghirlandaio, Filippino Lippi, Gerolamo di Benvenuto, Vittore Carpaccio, and Michele da Verona. The predominance of mythological themes on these *cassoni*—part of the general process of secularizing culture completed in the sixteenth century—serves to remind one again of the lively inspiration which the early Renaissance found in that fascinating mantle of legend and lore which the ancient Greeks wove around their land and embodied in their literature and their artistic creations, and which from them became an integral part of the literature and art of the entire West, ancient and modern.

Ovid was a never-failing source of inspiration for the artists in this field, though Homer, Vergil, Livy, Hyginus, Plutarch, the *Gesta Romanorum,* Dante, Petrarch, and Boccaccio were all favorite sources which quickened the hands of the painters. And if the *cassone*-painter illustrates Homer, he does not as a rule compete with him or with Vergil. Ovid is closer to his heart and capacity. His work is designed for the adornment of miniatures. It carries no great burden of ideas or feeling. The increasing availability of classical texts, translations, and handbooks from the early presses also had a stimulating effect upon the painters of Renaissance Italy, though we must not bind the painters to a literal or slavish adherence to literary texts. Many of these artists came from very humble origin and had little or no formal education outside of their craft. Through travel and war a general diffusion of culture spread throughout Europe, and in the course of time significant schools of art grew in Flanders, Germany, Holland, England, Spain, and France.

The judgment of Paris is a commonly recurring theme on *cassoni.* An early version of this legend now forms a part of the collection of the Fogg Museum of Art at Harvard University. The painting is executed on a panel which may have been used to decorate a wall or as part of a piece of furniture. For lack of any better identification the artist has been called by Schubring the "Paris-Master."[59] He belongs to the fifteenth century and had a marked predilection for Greek mythology.

To the left of the olive tree in the center of the picture stand the three goddesses: Hera, Aphrodite with a rose in her hair, and Athena. Hera holds an apple inscribed with the Greek words meaning "to the fair one." Zeus with a crown on his head counsels them to go to Paris for judgment. On the right the goddesses stand before Paris, who now holds the apple.

A panel in Munich also depicts the judgment of Paris. It is attributed to the school of Filippino Lippi (1460-1505).[60] Here again the three goddesses come before Zeus for advice regarding the award of the golden apple. Paris on the left is attracted to the beautiful goddesses, but is held back by Oenone. In the foreground a fool with a drum makes some dogs dance. Mt. Ida forms a background, and the costumes are of the period.

Still another panel, now in London, portrays the judgment scene. It is the work of Michele da Verona of the beginning of the sixteenth century,[61] who was a prolific painter of *cassoni* with subjects taken from classical history and mythology. The panel may have served as a wall decoration. In the background there is a fine stretch of mountain landscape which may have derived from the environs of Verona.

Other renderings of the same mythological theme, by the same "Paris-Master" referred to above, and by others, may be found in the volumes of Schubring.[62] The goddesses are sometimes shown in contemporary costume, or sometimes nude or draped. In one, Aphrodite is nude, but the other two goddesses are dressed like the Italian nobility.

A few other stories from the Trojan legend as found on *cassoni* may be mentioned here:[63] Achilles and Briseis; Briseis before Agamemnon; a group of Venus, Paris, and Helen; a group of Juno, Menelaus, and Athena; Thetis and Achilles; Achilles and Hector; the wooden horse before Troy; the banquet of Dido and Aeneas at which Dido heard recounted the story of Troy's fall; Peleus and Thetis;[64] Penthesilea; the fall of Troy; the Trojan horse; and the death of Hector.

JUDGMENT OF PARIS.—The judgment of Paris has been a favorite theme among painters of all ages. Details in some of these paintings are in the spirit of Greek antiquity; in others there is no attempt to conceal the artist's contemporary environment. There are early versions of this subject associated with the schools of the Florentine Cosimo Rosselli (c. 1439-1507), of the Venetian Vittore Carpaccio (c. 1455-1526), and attributed to the Sienese Pietro di Domenico (1457-1506).[65] There are also versions of the story painted by Paolo Veronese (1528-1588) in a private collection in London, and by Guido Reni (1575-1642) in the Hermitage at Leningrad. This story was commonly used by painters all over Europe.

A few versions of it by later painters are highly prized. Paintings of the story by Rubens (1577-1640) may be found in Dresden, the National Gallery in London, and Madrid. Rubens' rendering of this story is thought to be one of his greatest accomplishments. The effect of classical antiquity may be seen only in the nude figures, and even in form the goddesses are far from Greek. In the Flemish tradition in painting the female nude is not customary, but Rubens delighted in it. The central figure among the three goddesses is his young blond wife, whom as a girl of sixteen he married when he was fifty-three. In the painting's rich sensuousness of color and in the lusty, frankly exuberant beauty of the three goddesses may be seen something of the glowing, joyous satisfaction with life which marked the painter's last years. He need now no longer be afraid; life could not harm him. Imagination need not supply, for all was at hand. Hence the abundant and otiose trimmings: little Cupid, a peacock snarling at a dog, and an owl sitting wide awake in a tree. The painting is, as it should be, revealingly autobiographical.

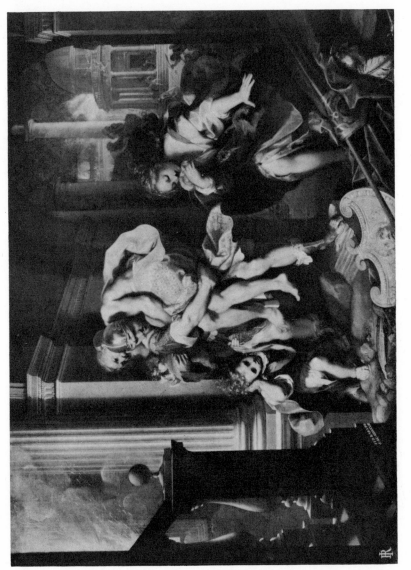

Baroccio. *The Burning of Troy*. Borghese Gallery, Rome. See page 115

The quarrel of Achilles and Agamemnon. Tapestry. Paris. See page 121

There are also versions of the judgment of Paris by the landscape painter, Claude Lorrain (1600-1682) in the Dalkeith Palace in Scotland; by the Dutch painter, Berchem (1620-1683) in Vienna; by Luca Giordano (1632-1705) in Berlin, Copenhagen, and Leningrad;[66] by Adrian van der Werff (1659-1722) in the Dulwich Gallery outside of London and in Dresden; by Antoine Watteau (1684-1721) (largely a study of the nude back of Venus) in the Louvre; by the German Mengs (1728-1779) (who spent many happy years in Rome) in the Hermitage at Leningrad; and by Jean Regnault (1754-1829). In the painting of Luca Giordano mentioned in the above list the romantic element enters in the person of Cupid, who draws his bow in mid-air. The French painter François Boucher (1703-1770), sometimes called the Anacreon of painting, for his graceful, decorative, and voluptuous style, made a canvas portraying Venus as she prepared for the judgment.[67]

ABDUCTION OF HELEN.—The abduction of Helen from her home in Sparta is another popular subject among painters. To Benozzo Gozzoli of the fifteenth century, who was responsible for the most important work done in the Campo Santo at Pisa, is attributed a wooden panel in the National Gallery in London bearing a delightful interpretation of the abduction of Helen by Paris. This ingenuous Florentine walked in the shadow of Giotto's campanile, saw the building of Brunelleschi's dome on the Cathedral and the beginning of Donatello's brilliant career, and became the favorite pupil of Fra Angelico. Hero and heroine are dressed as Florentine nobility. Amid a considerable entourage of knights and ladies Paris carries Helen from a charming palace of the Renaissance style to the waiting ships. The heroine in flowing robes sits on Paris' shoulders and clasps his neck with her arms. The simple faith of this Florentine artist naturally spared Helen any sense of guilt or violence and the course of the group leads across a flowering meadow toward a sunny lake lying under a range of smiling hills.

In Settignano there is what in all likelihood is another version of the abduction of Helen, by an Italian artist of the same versatility as Leonardo da Vinci and a passionate lover of the Classics, Francesco di Giorgio (1439-1502). His painting is a good example of the sweetness and vitality of the classical tradition in the hands of these artists of the *quattrocento*.[68] Then there are other romantic versions of the same subject by the illustrious Raphael (1483-1520) in a fresco which was once placed over a door in the Villa Raphael in Rome, but which is now in Leningrad; by Giulio Romano (*c.* 1492-1546) (generally considered to be Raphael's best pupil) in Mantua; and by Guido Reni, in Rome and in the Louvre. Guido Reni's version of this story is pretty and quiet. A benign Helen is gently led away by Paris amid a group of ladies and warriors. An atmosphere of playfulness is established by a torchbearing Cupid flying through the air, a pretty little Cupid with bow and arrows, a playful puppy, and a servant boy with a monkey on a string.

FLIGHT OF AENEAS.—Another frequently recurring subject is the flight of Aeneas from Troy. Luca Signorelli (*c.* 1441-*c.* 1523) has a version of this subject in fresco in the Academy at Siena. Raphael painted in fresco on the wall of one of the apartments in the Vatican the fire in the Leonine City in Rome in the year 847. In the background Pope Leo IV may be seen on the loggia of the palace arresting the advancing flames with a benediction. In the foreground Raphael inserted, as a tribute to the ancient tradition, a fleeing family. A distracted and exhausted old man is being carried from the disaster on the shoulders of his heroic and valiant son. They are accompanied by a barefoot lady from behind and by a child in front. If

Raphael's famous biographer Vasari was reminded of Vergil, we may be, too.

In the Borghese Gallery in Rome is *The Burning of Troy* of Baroccio (Federico Fiori, 1528-1612) fellow townsman of Raphael and friend of Michelangelo. The central subject of this vivid painting is the dramatic flight of Aeneas with his father, wife, and child from the burning city. Though the characters are portrayed in ancient dress, yet the architectural setting is of the Renaissance. The dome on the circular temple in the background reminds one of St. Peter's, the dome of which was completed a scant decade before this painting, which is dated as of 1598, in the seventieth year of the artist.

In Munich are two versions by Brueghel and Elsheimer, painters of the sixteenth century, of the flight of Aeneas from the destruction of Troy. In the Louvre, Lionello Spada (1576-1622) has a painting of Aeneas and Anchises; and in Madrid there is *The Flight of Aeneas from Troy* by Luca Giordano.

HISTORICAL BACKGROUND.—The preceding pages contain abundant evidence of the interest of the Italian artists in classical mythology, and of their capacity to re-create it. An earmark of their work is their joyous spontaneity. Before leaving these artists it would be well to look at the background of their times. This flourishing of the arts in Italy was one of the by-products of a peaceful Italy during most of the second half of the fifteenth century. By contrast, however, the period of 1492-1516 was for Italy one of strife, spoliation, and dissipation of her resources from within and without, devastation of her cities and finally enslavement to foreign powers. Alexander VI brought to Rome Pinturicchio and Michelangelo and to the papacy greed and worldliness. Julius II was a patron of the arts and at the same time the scourge of Italy. Great art continued to flourish in this period of decline partly out of sheer inertia. Bramante died in 1514 and Raphael in

1520; Rome was sacked in 1527 and Florence fell in 1530. The main force of the Italian Renaissance was spent. But prostrate Italy was to become a school for the rest of the Continent. In France, where there had been little painting prior to the year 1515 by Frenchmen, the new royal château was being built at Fontainebleau; and in 1533 the second son of Francis I, later to come to the throne as Henry II, was married to Catherine de' Medici. He worked untiringly for the encouragement of the arts, which served the King and his court. The next generation saw an influx of Italians (mostly Florentines) into France to perpetuate their growing mediocrity there and present France with an art which her artists could resent more easily than surpass. The tradition of Italian painters in France included such painters as Leonardo da Vinci, Andrea del Sarto, Primaticcio, and Luca Penni. One of the paintings left by Primaticcio at Fontainebleau was his *Paris Wounded before the Walls of Troy*. In the Louvre is a spirited version by Luca Penni of the Trojans bringing the wooden horse within the walls.[69] Italian humanists, invited to Germany by Maximilian, helped to create there, too, a renaissance of the arts and a unified German people. If time and historical circumstance dulled the freshness of these artists of the late Renaissance, at least they learned to be academic, descriptive, and entertaining. The ornamental prettiness of the romantic love embodied in their work adorned many a royal wall, has preserved a record of the outer graces of the time, and serves as a cosmetic to a relationship between the sexes which was none too healthy at that time.

GENERAL INTEREST, AFTER ITALIAN RENAISSANCE.—Additional paintings on Trojan themes prior to the neoclassical revival of the eighteenth century are indicative of current interest in the Trojan legend in Italy and throughout Europe as the warmth of the Italian Renaissance pervaded the Continent. Only a few of these need be mentioned in this work.

In the Borghese Museum in Rome is *Vulcan's Forge and Venus the Victorious* of Francesco Albani (1578-1660), a close friend of Guido Reni.

Sebastiano Ricci (1662-1734) painted *The Sacrifice of Polyxena at the Tomb of Achilles,* which is in the Louvre.

A version of the building of the Trojan horse by Giovanni Battista Tiepolo (*c.* 1696-1770), a Venetian artist, was on exhibition in 1940 at the great International Exposition. Its permanent home is in London. Tiepolo painted with an operatic abandon. In his painting the great wooden frame of the horse is being energetically pushed to completion. On the side stand Agamemnon and Odysseus, the latter in a disguise which he had once used when entering Troy before its fall. Vultures soar ominously over the city.[70] Two other interpretations of the introduction of the horse into Troy by the same artist—one in London and one in Paris—show his interest in letting his imagination play upon the subject. Tiepolo also painted in fresco in the Villa Valmarana at San Sebastiano near Vicenza two scenes based upon passages in the *Iliad,* portraying Athena hindering Achilles from slaying Agamemnon, and Briseis being carried away from Achilles and led to Agamemnon.[71] The Royal Palace in Madrid also has a painting by Tiepolo called *Aeneas Conducted by Venus to the Temple of Immortality,*[72] and the Brussels Museum has his *The Sacrifice of Polyxena.*[73]

*The Death of Laocoön* by El Greco (*c.* 1545-1614) is in Munich. This artist's admiration for Greece is evident in his name.

In the Louvre there is a painting by Claude Lorrain called *Ulysses Restoring Chryseis,* the latter being the maiden over whose return to her home arose the quarrel between Agamemnon and Achilles at the opening of the *Iliad.* This French artist, having spent many years in Rome, thought the dignity of classic structure a necessary complement to his scene.

In the Museum at Rheims is a painting of Mathieu Le Nain (1607-1677), his *Venus at the Forge of Vulcan.*

The Prado Gallery in Madrid has a version in contemporary dress of Vulcan at his forge, by Rubens.

Evidence of the arrival of the classical influence in Holland is clear in the version of the wedding of Peleus and Thetis by the Dutch painter Abraham Bloemaert (1564-1651), whose studies had taken him to Paris.

The *Homer* of Rembrandt (1606-1669) representing the aged bard dictating his poems is in the Royal Picture Gallery at The Hague.

Finally, the Turin Gallery has an *Oenone and Paris* by Adrian van der Werff.

## TAPESTRY

SOURCES OF LEGENDS ON TAPESTRY AND EXTENT OF TAPESTRY WEAVING.—The weaving of tapestries is another of the sister arts which developed throughout Europe during and since the Renaissance. Its story in any one period cannot be written apart from the history, the literature, and other arts of the time, for example, painting, fresco, and the making of illuminated manuscripts. All the arts of a given age are manifestations of a dominant enthusiasm which seeks expression through them. An inventory of the late fifteenth century of the House of Burgundy refers to seventeen manuscripts relating to the story of Troy. A preponderant number of them undoubtedly were based ultimately on mediaeval sources. Literary interests of this type—and they will have to be assumed for most of Europe—inevitably found expression in the manufacture of tapestries, as in the other arts. Painters, too, with their absorbing interest in classical legend, could not fail to influence to a marked degree the hands of contemporary weavers. On occasion painters were commissioned to make the cartoons from which tapestries were made. In other cases the customary exhibitions or salons provided the inspiration which led to reproductions of paintings in tapestry. Some of the creations of the Gobelins establishment in Paris came out of contemporary paintings. This house became the leading center in Europe for the weaving of large hangings. Hundreds of manufactories grew up in every country on the Continent and in the British Isles; and their story and work constitute another chapter in the cultural history of, among other nations, France, Germany, England, Holland, Belgium, Italy, Spain, Scotland, Sweden, and Ireland—from the fourteenth century down to modern times. The golden age of tapestry was in the last quarter of the fifteenth century. The weaving of tapestries flourished in such centers as Arras, a city of northern France, in the fourteenth and fifteenth centuries, whence our word "arras" meaning "tapestry"; Brussels in the fifteenth and sixteenth centuries; Paris in the sixteenth and seventeenth; and Mortlake, just outside of London, in the seventeenth. These tapestries survive in collections and exhibitions in hundreds of museums, palaces, cathedrals, salons, and galleries, public and private, all over the world today. Here again the Renaissance had an opportunity to develop its skills and both to see and express its own absorbing enthusiasms in classical mythology.

TROJAN LEGEND ON TAPESTRIES.—With the Trojan legend holding its prominent place in the other artistic forms of those centuries, especially in painting, which is the art most closely allied to the art of weaving, it follows of necessity that the tapestry weavers would not neglect the legend, either. In fact, the most numerous and familiar scenes of romantic heroes and battles shown on tapestries are derived from the Trojan

War. A striking feature of tapestries is the constant recurrence of this most familiar of legends. The method in tapestry of depicting the costume and setting of the legends is much the same as the method in painting. The stories may be retold in terms of the scene contemporary to the artist, or some approximation of what was regarded as ancient setting may be attempted. The latter is evident more often in the eighteenth century, and the former in the Renaissance.

In the Romance countries there is ample evidence of the hold of the Trojan legend upon the imaginations of the creators of tapestries. Nicolas Bataille, in 1376, sold to Louis I, Duke of Anjou, a high-loom tapestry portraying the story of Hector. Philip the Bold (1342-1404) is known to have had a tapestry, bought in 1386, portraying the story of the golden apple. An inventory of the tapestries owned by the Duke of Orléans consists in the main of tapestries made before the year 1400; among them are mentioned seven large old tapestries on the destruction of Troy. In 1472 the city of Bruges bought a tapestry of the destruction of Troy. Henry VII of England (1457-1509) in 1488 also bought eleven pieces of tapestry on Troy. A tapestry from the Abruzzi of the early Renaissance portraying the Trojan horse will be found reproduced in Schubring's treatise on *cassoni*.[74] In this tapestry prehistoric Troy has been made over into a mediaeval castle. It happens to be one of the few surviving early links between tapestry and *cassoni*.

A tapestry of Norwegian manufacture of the period around 1580, portraying the abduction of Helen, is at Oslo.[75] Again, costumes, setting, and characters are contemporary rather than ancient. The abundance of Trojan tapestries and their geographical spread in these early times is indicative of the extent to which the literary tradition of the Trojan legend had penetrated into the popular consciousness.

# PAINTING, CERAMICS, AND TAPESTRY

Aubusson in the center of France was the seat of celebrated weavers of tapestry from the early sixteenth century. Here about the year 1650 was made a tapestry of the judgment of Paris.[76] The background is one of French castles and landscape. The characters are in French dress. Paris, dressed as a French peasant, extends the apple to Venus as her gift. The deities are French matrons rather than Greek goddesses.

The banquet of Dido and Aeneas, at which the tale of Troy's fall was related, is elaborately portrayed in another tapestry of the middle of the seventeenth century.[77]

A generation later a tapestry of the flight of Aeneas from the destruction of Troy was made at Aubusson.[78] Aeneas is portrayed in his familiar rôle of carrying the aged Anchises on his back from the burning city. Ascanius, holding his father by the hand, goes on ahead. The Trojan horse stands on rollers in the background. In this tapestry, too, the costumes and setting are of the contemporary rather than of the ancient period.

In 1723 Charles Coypel, understudy of his father, Antoine, added one piece to a set of five tapestries in illustration of the *Iliad* which his father had made in 1717.

A magnificent tapestry in Paris depicts the dramatic story of the quarrel of Achilles and Agamemnon over Briseis. An approximation of ancient costume is attempted in this tapestry. It came out of the Gobelins establishment in Paris, and belongs to the period 1721-1725.[79]

The amorous relations of the deities, Venus and Vulcan, were woven, in 1774, into another tapestry of this manufactory.[80] The vogue and taste of the time explain the nude Venus and ornamental Cupids.

Out of Beauvais, a center of weaving inaugurated at the same time as the revival of the Gobelins manufactory in Paris, about the year 1765 came a tapestry showing the abduction of Helen.[81] Helen is depicted as being escorted to a boat from

the walls of her city. She is accompanied by the usual ornamental flying Cupids of the eighteenth century in France.
The spirit of this tapestry is genteel, romantic, and lively,
and the costumes are in ancient style. The architectural
background has Greek, Roman, and Egyptian elements in it.

For the palace at Chantilly, in 1802, there was reproduced
the painting of Vien, *Briseis Led from the Tent of Achilles*
(1781). Other paintings of Vien, Suvée, Vincent, Callet,
Garnier, Guérin, and Boucher were reproduced in tapestry.[82]

Because of the surviving examples it is clear that the tapestry
weavers shared in the neoclassical renaissance which swept
through Italy and France in the late eighteenth century.

RENAISSANCE TAPESTRIES ON WARS OF TROY.—From the
fifteenth century more than a dozen pieces of different sets
of tapestries portraying the Wars of Troy still survive. Most
of them are in the Cathedral of Zamorra in Spain, in the
Victoria and Albert Museum in London, in the museum of
Berne, Switzerland, in Paris, and in private collections in
America. These constitute the most important collection of
Gothic historical tapestries in existence. They are magnificent
exhibitions of the skill of designer and weaver alike, and in
composition and workmanship they portray with photographic realism and fidelity the contemporary military
customs and costumes of a people whose absorbing interest
was the portrayal of warfare.

The original sketches from which the cartoons of these sets
are thought to have been made, dating in the third quarter of
the fifteenth century, were discovered and were published in
1898. They were made by the now eminently regarded French
painter, illuminator, and miniaturist, Jean Foucquet (*c.* 1415-
1480), a master artist even among masters. Now in the
Louvre, they are known by the name of their former owner,
"Schumann" drawings. The general uniformity of spirit and

story of these drawings suggests a common literary source, and some suggest that they were made in the same school. In the light of the literary tradition of the story of Troy, down through the Middle Ages to the Renaissance, one would hardly expect the early weavers of tapestry to derive their inspiration directly from the pure tradition of Homer himself. As a matter of fact, the story told on these tapestries is far more inclusive than the *Iliad* and the *Odyssey,* and different from them, going back to the first Greek expedition against Troy, and to the destruction of Troy. Benoit may be regarded as the ultimate source for the stories woven into these tapestries.

There are two pieces of tapestry in America containing scenes from the earlier Greek expedition against Troy. They are in all likelihood part of a once complete series depicting the tale of Troy as told by Benoit. The legend goes that Heracles and Jason, while on the Argonautic expedition, stopped at Troy, which was then under the rule of Laomedon. While there, Heracles rescued Hesione, Laomedon's daughter, from a sea monster. Laomedon promised Heracles a reward, but later peremptorily dismissed him from the city. After the completion of the Argonautic expedition Heracles returned to Troy with a group of heroes, slew Laomedon and all his sons, except Priam, and destroyed the city. One of these pieces of tapestry shows Heracles and Jason arriving at Troy to punish Laomedon, and the other shows Heracles holding the head of the decapitated king in his left hand.[88] The former piece was woven at Tournai about the year 1475 by Jean Le Quien III. Other scenes portrayed on these sets of the Wars of Troy, some pieces of which are in private collections in America, are the embassy of Antenor to Greece, Odysseus and Diomedes at the court of Priam, Hector, and Andromache (perhaps the finest Trojan tapestry in America), the slaying of Patroclus by Hector, the death and funeral of Hector, the deaths of Achilles,

Paris, and Penthesilea, the "fifth column" activities of Antenor in betrayal of his country, the wooden horse, the capture of Troy, the slaying of Priam, and the burning of Troy.

Five hangings from this set of tapestries on the Wars of Troy are known to have once adorned the walls of the Westminster Palace. Stripped from the walls in 1800, they later were sold at virtually the price of old rags. They are, however, survived by a series of drawings of them, now in the Victoria and Albert Museum, made by a contemporary architect. The fact that there is only an occasional correspondence between these drawings and those in the Louvre mentioned above indicates once again the freedom with which the tapestry weavers worked.[84]

Another tapestry from the set on the Wars of Troy, woven at Tournai in the second half of the fifteenth century, and now in the Victoria and Albert Museum, has three scenes,[85] as follows: Penthesilea, the Amazon queen, joining the Trojans; the same queen vanquishing Diomedes; and the investiture of Pyrrhus. In the upper left corner appear the battlemented walls of Troy with three gates, as though the city were a feudal castle. On the left of the main body of the tapestry a cortège of Trojans and Amazons approach Priam as he stands in the courtyard. Penthesilea, kneeling, offers to him her aid. One of the Amazons holds the train of the queen's sumptuous robe, which she wears above her armor. Standing close to Priam are Antenor and Aeneas. In the middle of the tapestry the Trojans, under the leadership of Penthesilea, pour from the gate of the city against the Greeks. In the fury of the battle Penthesilea, who has unhorsed Diomedes, wields her sword triumphantly over him. On the right Pyrrhus, who is destined to slay the Amazon queen, stands before the tent of his father Achilles, clad in mediaeval armor, as are all the warriors of the piece. Ajax is putting a sword belt on him. Two other tapestries of this set on the Trojan Wars are in Paris.[86]

TAPESTRIES OF BRITISH ISLES.—King James IV in preparation for his wedding, in 1503, made several purchases of tapestries. For the wedding the King's Hall at Holyrood House in Edinburgh was hung with the *Story of Old Troy*, and another room was hung with the *History of Troy*. Out of this wedlock the Stuart dynasty came to the throne of England.

Henry VIII (1491-1547) is known through an inventory taken after his death to have had at Otelands nine pieces of tapestry on the story of Troy; at Westminster, eleven different pieces on the story of Hector, six on Helen and Paris, and seven on the story of Vulcan, Mars, and Venus; and at Windsor, eleven on the siege of Troy. The same inventory reveals (at Hampton Court) two pieces of arras on the story of Aeneas.

An inventory of furnishings at Holyrood House in the reign of Mary Queen of Scots (1542-1587) included eight pieces on the judgment of Paris and eight on the sailing of Aeneas. Another rendering of the judgment of Paris, around 1595, is in the Victoria and Albert Museum in London.[87]

In the period 1630-1635 the painter Rubens drew the cartoons for a series of tapestries on the story of Achilles, thus contributing to that fine period when the manufactory at Mortlake had no rival. One piece of this series is now in the Boston Museum of Fine Arts.[88]

A sale of the royal collections in the period 1649-1653 has left a record of five pieces of arras at Whitehall on the story of Aeneas and twelve at Windsor on the siege of Troy.

In the seventeenth century, in Scotland, the Earl of Dunfermline had in his possession ten old and worn pieces of tapestry on the stories of Aeneas, Troy, and Mankind.

Knowing about these tapestries leaves with one a sense of the importance of the Trojan legend in the history of the time-honored craft of tapestry weaving, and of its dependence on literature and painting and its complement to the traditions of both literature and painting.

## NEOCLASSICAL SCHOOL OF PAINTING
### ESPECIALLY IN FRANCE

ORIGIN AND EVALUATION—The Neoclassical School of French painters, foremost among whom are Vien, David, and Guérin, brings us to a new appreciation of the ancient classical world in general and then, under the added impetus of the Romantic movement at the end of the eighteenth century, to an idealized and sentimentalized Hellenism. New vistas into the ancient world had been opened up, after 1738, by the discoveries at Herculaneum and Pompeii, by the writings of Winckelmann, and by the marked advances of French classical scholarship. In 1793, the Louvre was established, and during the next decade Napoleon acquired for that museum countless artistic treasures. With regard to the long tradition of classical scholarship in France, in the seventeenth century Racine, himself the pupil of distinguished French classicists, had read widely in the ancient Greek and Latin classics, and was especially devoted to Sophocles and Euripides, though his plays are really children of the psychology of his day. An outstanding monument of French scholarship of the eighteenth century is Barthélémy's *Voyages du jeune Anacharsis* (1789) a work which occupied a full generation of the author's life. It is, in a fictional setting, a scholarly synthesis of all the knowledge at that time available regarding the various phases of Greek culture. Within ten years of its first appearance it went through six editions, and was translated into several languages, enriching the present wherever it went with a better understanding of Greek culture. Its glorification of Greek democratic ideas and ideals exerted an influence during the French Revolution. Thanks to this distinguished tradition of

French scholarship, which also included the names of Budaeus, the Stephani, Lambinus, and Montaigne, the ancient authors provided corresponding fairways in the realm of human dignity and personal and social freedom. And so the full effect of the art and thought of classical antiquity fell upon French painting in the late eighteenth century and brought it into a period of imitation and academic re-creation of the Greek and Roman past.

This period of neoclassical revival, like the corresponding periods which developed in other countries, crystallized both French painting and the Classics for a half century at a point short of their total capacities. The total effect is that derived from looking at a convincing corpse. The best of ancient Greek art at this time was either not yet discovered, or if discovered, was not perfectly appraised or available. Great admiration was felt for the art of Greek decline or for Roman copies of dubious relationship to their Greek originals. The French artists were interested in the human figure, idealized and static, either in the nude or draped. Background, mattering little, was conventional; emotions were ignored; rules were important. A symbol of this period of imitation and partial reproduction of the classical spirit is, the German painter, Antony Raphael Mengs (1728-1779), who spent much of his life in Rome. Eighteenth century France was an age of artificiality and mannerism, and the artificiality of having classic ruins thrust into French landscapes and classic legends deployed against a background of Versailles architecture is in line with other affectations of the time. And yet the final effect of these artists is not completely un-French or merely academic. For in their work are French grace and chivalry, French landscape, occasionally, French scholarly comprehension, and French heroism and patriotism in the face of oppression.

Vien.—There are two paintings of the French artist Vien

(1716-1809) in the Museum at Angers: *Briseis Led from the Tent of Achilles,* which was reproduced in tapestry for the Palace at Chantilly in 1802, and *The Return of Priam with the Body of Hector.* At Alger is Vien's *Departure of Priam after the Death of Hector,* to which his painting at Angers is a complement. He also made an etching of the death of Patroclus. At Rouen may be seen his *The Anger of Achilles,* and at Épinal, *The Parting of Hector and Andromache.* The time of Vien's youth had witnessed a new appreciation of Homer.

Indeed, the art of the early eighteenth century, encouraged by the Court, was predominantly mythological, though Madame de Pompadour expressed a weariness of ancient themes and heroes, and wished to make French art contemporary in theme.

The Comte de Caÿlus (1692-1765) an antiquarian, man of letters, engraver, and adventurer, is distinguished for his ardent interest in classical antiquities and his admiration for Homer and Vergil. He traveled widely in Italy, Greece, and the East; visited Troy; and published extensively in the field of classical antiquities. In his correspondence and in two volumes on his field of interest he suggested the *Iliad,* the *Odyssey,* and the *Aeneid* as better sources than Ovid for painters and sculptors. Both painters and weavers of tapestry had been, even if to a comparatively small degree, anticipating his suggestion for a half century. His interest in the young Vien undoubtedly contributed to Vien's attraction to classical subjects.

To the school of Vien belongs François Vincent (1746-1816), who put upon canvas an ancient story, known to Cicero and the Elder Pliny, that the Greek painter Zeuxis made a painting of Helen through a synthesis of five nude models whom the people of Croton supplied for him. In this painting of 1789 (in the Louvre) Zeuxis chooses the girls of Croton who will serve as models.

David. *Paris and Helen*. Louvre, Paris. See page 130

Ingres. *The Apotheosis of Homer.* Louvre, Paris. See page 131

# PAINTING, CERAMICS, AND TAPESTRY

DAVID.—Jacques Louis David (1748-1825), a student of Vien, may be regarded as the founder of the French Neo-classical School. As a youth he had in school a smattering of the Classics. But when his artistic talents were recognized, he was apprenticed to Vien, the pioneering admirer of the classical tradition. Following the spirit of his teacher he won the *prix de Rome* with a classical subject. With the appointment of Vien as director of the French Academy at Rome both teacher and pupil went to the eternal city. The way had been marvelously prepared for them by Winckelmann, who though now dead, during the preceding two decades had through his studies and publications on ancient art created an intense interest in the art and ideals of ancient Greece and Rome. A new interest in Homer arose through Winckelmann's citation of Homer as the ultimate source of inspiration of many pieces of art. Besides, the growing Vatican Museum had a profoundly molding effect on those who came to see its treasures. The man who had suggested its establishment, Pius VI, was now Pope. The opening of this and other museums both in Italy and throughout Europe was prompted by accumulating discoveries of antiquities at Pompeii, in the Campagna, and in Etruria.

And so David's devotion to the art and thought of ancient Rome was the most formative influence of his life and career. His drawings of classical works often found their way bodily into his paintings. When David returned to Paris he found himself not only painter to Louis XVI, but also the very fountainhead of a new wave of extravagant admiration of ancient culture and ideals. Many of his paintings were designed to instill in their observers some of the more severe social disciplines and attitudes coming out of the ancient world, and were both products and symbols of the rapidly moving social upheaval of their immediate environment. When the French

Revolution broke in 1789 in the wake and after the pattern of the American Revolution some fifteen years before, the whole of France, but especially David, tingled with that same idealism which, instilled in the hearts of the fathers of American independence through their study of the Classics, became enshrined in the Constitution of the United States and inspired the most constructive generation in American history.[89]

The following works of this famous French painter are especially worthy of mention: a pen drawing of the funeral ceremonies of Patroclus (in the Louvre); *The Grief of Andromache over the Death of Hector* (at the École des Beaux Arts, Paris), the exhibition of which in the salon of 1785 marked the beginning of the cold, disengaged, scholarly art of neoclassicism; the *Paris and Helen* with its exquisite classical atmosphere (in the Louvre); and finally *The Combat of Minerva against Mars and Venus* (in the Louvre) a painting in reminiscence, perhaps, of passages in the fifth and twenty-first books of the *Iliad,* where all three divinities contend.[90]

INGRES.—Ingres (1780-1867) a student of David, became in his day the leader of the French Neoclassical School, although he once said, when asked about the source for his horses of Napoleon's chariot, that they came from Phidias and the bus horses! His remark shows his independence of tradition. He was also a close student and admirer of Raphael. With *The Arrival of Agamemnon's Ambassadors at the Tent of Achilles* (in the École des Beaux Arts) Ingres won the *prix de Rome* in 1801 and the high praise and friendship of the English designer Flaxman, who will be found, by way of poetic justice, among the figures in the right foreground of Ingres' later painting, *The Apotheosis of Homer.* His quarter century of residence among the art treasures of antiquity and of the Renaissance in Italy filled him with reverence and inspiration. In Basel is his *Venus Wounded by Diomedes,* a reminiscence of that scene in the fifth book of the *Iliad* where the goddess while protecting Aeneas is wounded by the Greek warrior Diomedes. In making this work Ingres was also influenced by Flaxman's drawings in illustration of Homer. At Aix-en Provence is his portrayal of *Jupiter Supplicated by Thetis* (1817).[91] A well-known work of Ingres is his (1827) *Apotheosis of Homer* (in the Louvre). The original painting was made to adorn the ceiling of the Gallery of Charles X in the Louvre. The blind Homer, seated before the threshold of the temple dedicated to him, is crowned with a wreath by the goddess of Victory. He receives the homage of the poets, artists, and orators grouped around him, one of whom extends to him his lyre. At his feet sit his two daughters: the *Iliad* on our left clothed in red and as though startled into attention, and the *Odyssey* on our right clothed in green and in a mood of pensive reflection. For the central idea of his theme Ingres is indebted to Raphael's *School of Athens*. In the arches of the ceiling on either side of his original painting Ingres painted two other scenes in tribute to Homer: *Apollo Crowning the Iliad and the Odyssey*, and *Seven Cities Claim the Birth of Homer*. He also painted *Homer and his Guide*, which is in a private collection of the royal family of Belgium.[92]

OTHER CONTEMPORARY FRENCH PAINTERS.—A few more paintings, illustrating the Trojan legend, by French artists of the time will now be mentioned. In the salon of 1800 was exhibited *The Desolation of Priam's Family* by Étienne Garnier (1759-1849) portraying the despair of Priam's family when watching the outraging of Hector's corpse by Achilles from the walls of Troy, a painting which later was reproduced in tapestry. One of the last of the direct followers of David and his classical tendencies was François Gérard (1770-1837) who made at Caen a portrait of Homer, an *Achilles and Patroclus*, and at Tarbes, an *Achilles Finding the Body of*

*Patroclus.* The *Andromache and Pyrrhus* (in the Louvre) of
Pierre Guérin (1774-1833) pupil of Jean Regnault and one of
the most confirmed neoclassicists of the period, brought him
considerable acclaim. In this painting Pyrrhus extends his
protection to the Trojan lady, who kneels before him. In the
salon of 1817 he presented his *Aeneas Relating to Dido the
Disasters of Troy*, which is also in the Louvre.[93] Then there is
Jérôme Langlois (1779-1838), who made two paintings on the
Trojan legend: *Priam at the Feet of Achilles* (1809) and
*Cassandra Imploring the Vengeance of Minerva* (1817).

FUSELI.—Parts of this neoclassical environment in England
were Wedgwood's pottery and the painter and lecturer, Henry
Fuseli (1741-1825). By his extensive period of residence in
Italy (1770-1778) Fuseli followed the pattern of most artists
of his time. He developed a worshiping admiration for
Michelangelo and Homer. In his inner temperament he was,
and in his outer manners he sought to become, the Michelangelo of his day. His close knowledge of Homeric Greek won
him the esteem of Cowper, who was then translating Homer
and who often availed himself of Fuseli's help in this task.
With his paintings and hundreds of sketches he illustrated a
wide range of ancient and modern poetry, especially Homer.
A man with a keen admiration for the lofty and a flair for the
grand, he yet lacked the capacity for exacting self-discipline
in his profession, painting, as it were, with a floor mop. With
his impetuosity and depths of interest in the immortals of art
he was not perfectly born to a time when enthusiasm was
suspect and really great art disturbing.

## WEDGWOOD POTTERY

BACKGROUND OF WEDGWOOD'S INTEREST IN TROJAN
LEGEND. — One of the world's greatest potters, Josiah
Wedgwood (1730-1795) and his gifted collaborator John

Flaxman. *The Judgment of Paris.* Piroli engraving. Mayer Collection. See page 135

Leighton. *Captive Andromache*. Manchester. See page 136

Flaxman (1755-1826) applied their talent to a revival of classical forms and designs in ceramics. Flaxman as a young artist was employed originally by Wedgwood to make wax models of classical reliefs and vases. A mere glance at the dates of these two men will suffice to identify them at once with the eager interest in classical forms and ideals then prevalent throughout the Continent. Importations of ancient marbles, gems, and vases to the North grew apace, and the writings of Winckelmann spread abroad new knowledge and standards of appreciation of ancient art. Extensive discoveries in Etruria prompted Wedgwood to adopt the name *Etruria* for the home of his famous ware.

Enthusiasm for classical and especially Greek antiquity (as seen largely from Rome) brought together into rivalry and often into friendship (as in the case of Flaxman, Ingres, and David) artists, scholars, and travelers of many nationalities who in their travels became genuine ambassadors of good will among nations. Poet, painter, sculptor, and potter found in their pilgrimages to Rome an inspiration which carried their works, their fame, and themselves far and wide. So the humanizing influence of the arts helped to hold together a world torn apart by powerful forces which still today rock society to the very foundations.

LIMITATIONS OF THE EIGHTEENTH CENTURY POTTER.—In the Wedgwood potteries there lived once more in design and clay the exquisite grace, balance, and beauty, and the legends of classical art. Unfortunately, however, the genteel England of wigs and puffs in the eighteenth century was not prepared to recapture the genuine spirit of classical antiquity as easily as its outer forms and conventions. Greek art the age had to understand largely through Roman copies whose connection with Greek originals is still in many instances a matter of conjecture and theory. Flaxman's early youth was steeped in the Greek and Roman classics, but he could scarcely be expected to catch the great overtones of classical literature and art, even if his medium, concerned with the mechanical reproduction of small objects, had allowed. Homer is said to have been put into a wig by Pope and into a muslin dress by Flaxman. One must not expect the designer of vases to strive beyond the capacities of his medium, nor can all things be expected of any one age. No age has reproduced the Classics in their entirety, and ours, which could, neglects them. To this quiet, polite, English world the din of the French Revolution and of Beethoven's Fifth Symphony came as a noisy intrusion. But the limitations of the age and of the artistic medium need not affect one's appreciation of the true greatness of the artistic work of Wedgwood and Flaxman.

TROJAN LEGEND ON WEDGWOOD POTTERY.—When still in his early twenties Flaxman designed for Wedgwood a tablet with the judgment of Paris modeled on it in bas-relief. The tablet is of black jasper and the relief is white. The dimensions are approximately eighteen by seven inches. The exquisite modeling of the figures and draperies are worthy of note.

Not much later he designed a relief variously known as *The Apotheosis of Homer* and *The Crowning of a Kitharist,* a tablet in jasper ware now in the British Museum. This was a fine tribute to the poet who had inspired him from early childhood. Flaxman's graceful and simple design for this relief was based upon an ancient relief which was then in the Colonna Palace in Rome. There is also a black basalt vase with a design called *The Apotheosis of Homer* in the Victoria and Albert Museum. Another plaque, of blue jasper with white relief, in the same museum is by some regarded as *The Apotheosis of Vergil,* which Flaxman designed for Wedgwood.

About 1792, Flaxman made a series of drawings to illustrate the texts of Homer, thirty-nine for the *Iliad* and thirty-four for the *Odyssey*. Sixty-six of these are in the Diploma Gallery of the Royal Academy in London. Piroli engraved the plates of these drawings for the Rome edition of 1793, and between that time and 1882 these drawings were published in twenty-two different editions in London and other centers.

A few years before his death Flaxman undertook the laborious task of making drawings for a reproduction of the famous shield of Achilles as beautifully described in the eighteenth book of the *Iliad*. From these drawings now in the British Museum reproductions in low relief were made in silver gilt, bronze, and plaster. The qualities expressed in them, as in Flaxman's illustrations of the *Iliad* and *Odyssey*, are rather those of the eighteenth century than of heroic Greece. Other creations of the Wedgwood potteries were a vase of dark blue jasper in *crater* form with white bas-reliefs portraying Priam begging for the body of Hector, and Achilles with the daughters of Lycomedes, among whom he was hiding in order to avoid being drafted for service with the Greeks at Troy; also a large portrait bust of Homer in black basalt.[94]

## MODERN PAINTING

LEIGHTON, BURNE-JONES.—Sir Frederick Leighton (1830-1896) has won his laurels as a distinguished English painter. Two of his paintings within the scope of our subject are his *Helen on the Ramparts* and his *Captive Andromache*, at Manchester. His devotion to classical themes came out of a thorough grounding in the languages and the mythological lore of ancient Greece and Rome, instilled in him by his father, and out of his wide travels on the Continent in his father's company. His limitations, too, came out of his excessive schooling. He devoted his art only to noble and beautiful things. In the first of the paintings mentioned above, Helen advances along the ramparts of Troy accompanied by two handmaidens. The light, falling on her shoulder and neck, produces a beautiful silhouette of her. Her face, darkened by shadow, is heavy with a weary sadness. There is a mystical beauty in the picture, partly because of its sadness. Naturally, the inspiration for the painting came from the inimitable passage in the third book of the *Iliad* where Helen with the elders of Troy views the Greek forces from the wall. As for the *Captive Andromache*, Leighton presented it for exhibition at the Royal Academy in 1888. He had devoted much time in the years previous to that work, and it is one of the largest of his canvases. The theme was suggested to the artist by Elizabeth Browning's paraphrase of the words of Hector to his wife in the sixth book of the *Iliad:*

> that some stander-by,
> Marking thy tears fall, shall say, "This is She,
> The wife of that same Hector who fought best
> Of all the Trojans, when all fought for Troy."[95]

Andromache stands in line, clothed in black, waiting to fill her pitcher at a fountain (ordinarily the work of a servant). A restful family group in the foreground—a young mother resting her head on that of her husband, who kneels beside her, while their young baby, who sits erect on its mother's lap, fondles the cheek of its father—with its poignant reminder of a happiness that was once hers, causes Andromache to sob with bowed head. She has attracted the attention of a group of four in the foreground who look on her with pity. The coloring effects; the architectural background; the beauty of trees, mountain, and cloud; the truth and beauty of the use of drapery to conceal and yet to ennoble; and the general recreation of classical atmosphere are superb. One can come away from the painting a wiser and chastened person. In his dedication of his art to the beautiful and good; in the melancholy that comes from the juxtaposition of the beautiful and good with suffering; in his stress upon human beings as emotional and spiritual rather than intellectual creatures; in his interest in nature; and in his devotion to a Hellenism that included all the preceding Leighton is a product of his time. The Birmingham Art Gallery has two paintings by Sir Edward Burne-Jones (1833-1898) on Trojan themes: the *Story of Troy* and the *Helen Captive*. He, too, was an idealist and lover of beauty who established a deep spiritual kinship with the past and found new meaning in its legends, which were, so to speak, the conscience of its childhood.

FRENCH AND GERMAN PAINTERS. — In France, Henri Regnault (1843-1871) won the *grand prix* in 1866 with his forceful painting *Thetis Bringing the Arms Forged by Vulcan to Achilles*. Maignan (1845-1908) has left us his interpretation of the parting scene of Hector from his wife and child. In the Corcoran Gallery at Washington, D.C., there is a picture which made a sensation at its showing in the year 1874, *The Trojan Horse* by Henri Paul Motte (1846-1922). It was painted at a time when the minds of Frenchmen still lived under the shadow of the Franco-Prussian War of 1870-1872, and portrays with photographic and antiquarian realism the sabotage of Troy by the Greeks in the wooden horse. The setting of the painting is the citadel of Troy on the fateful night when the city was to fall by treachery from within and trust in the stranger. There is enough light for the huge bulk of the horse to cast its lowering shadow upon the battlement in the background. Greek warriors are sliding down a rope from the top of the horse and stealthily making their way down a staircase leading into the city. The body of a Trojan sentinel lies on the ground.[96]

In Brussels there is a fine painting by Wiertz (1806-1865) with the fight between the Greeks and the Trojans for the body of Patroclus as its subject. The National Gallery of Berlin has a version of the abduction of Helen painted by Rudolf von Deutsch. The characters are in ancient dress, but before the Romantic Movement a man could not carry off a lady as Paris does here. There is also in the painting a Teutonic emphasis upon masculine virility.

MODERN VERSIONS OF JUDGMENT OF PARIS.—Some other versions in modern times of the judgment of Paris are those of Alfred Stevens (1817-1875) in the Tate Gallery in London; Henry P. Gray (1819-1877) in the Corcoran Gallery in Washington; Fantin-Latour (1836-1904) at Rheims; Renoir (1841-1920) in several versions; the daring and eccentric German Max Klinger (1857-1920), who raised a furore in 1887 with his direct and unheroic painting of the story, which finally found a home in the Modern Gallery of Vienna;[97] Solomon J. Solomon (1860-1927);[98] René Ménard (1862-1930); and finally the Spaniard Mariano Andreü (born in 1888).

The first of these painters, Alfred Stevens, brought to his work an intimate knowledge of Italy from his long residence and study there. For a time he assisted Thorvaldsen. He was a man of large spiritual and professional stature, like some of the great Renaissance artists. In Solomon's romantic version Venus stands nude before an apple tree in full blossom, confidently displaying her youthful beauty, while Athena and Hera on either side of her look on admiringly. In the painting of Ménard, Paris offers the apple to Venus (they are both painted in the nude) in a pastoral setting of languid Vergilian peace and repose at the closing in of evening's shadows upon the countryside.[99] The painting of Andreü[100] is a study of poses. Paris, apple in hand, sits in the presence of the three nude goddesses. Venus, in the center, stands on a sea shell before a mirror which Cupid, poised in air, holds for her. On the left, Hera poses under a raised umbrella. On the right,

Athena, identified and clothed only by her helmet, lolls with unladylike ease on a waist-high column.

Modern painters have expressed themselves in a bewildering array of movements and countermovements like waves upon a choppy sea. Impressionism, neo-impressionism, academism, Fauvism, cubism (lyrical and methodical) purism, orphism, neocubism, realism, the new subjectivity, Dadaism, surrealism, neohumanism, impressionism, expressionism, and futurism all follow one upon the heels of another. All fill their canvases with an endless variety of female nudes in various poses, postures, and states of disarray. To judge them all would weary any judge and try any judgment. Paris will have to defer to Time itself.

# V. THE LEGEND IN SCULPTURE AND ON GEMS AND COINS

THE TROJAN LEGEND has had a long history in sculpture, both ancient and modern, despite the considerable number of competing subjects (dedicatory, religious, funerary, secular, and others) for which sculpture has provided a vehicle of expression. In none other of the arts is the information at hand to enable the tracing of a continuous story through the ages to the extent that this was possible with literature. In any important sense many of the manual skills lay undeveloped during the Middle Ages.

The Homeric poems and those of the epic cycle provided the early sculptors of Greece with an unparalleled narrative of heroic adventure and a tantalizing repertoire of heroes and heroines for translation into marble and bronze, once the necessary technical skill was acquired. It will be noticed in this as in other arts that with regard to ultimate epic sources no particular partiality for Homer will be evident in antiquity to the exclusion of the epic cycle. In fact, in the archaic artistic work of Greece certain parts of the Trojan legend outside the Homeric poems proved more popular than either the *Iliad* or the *Odyssey*.

The history of Greek sculpture, whatever its subject matter, is the story of artists growing in ability to express their ideals and their conception of life, through sculpture as easily as through words. In Greek sculpture at its best the artist developed a unique willingness to allow his hand to accept the

Motte. *The Trojan Horse.* Courtesy of the Corcoran Gallery, Washington. See page 137

Relief of Paris, Eros, Aphrodite, Helen, Peitho. Naples. See page 144

discipline imposed by the mind and to allow the mind to respond to the haunting sense of an ideal esthetic beauty in the human body as envisioned in the imagination. Greek sculpture in its full maturity added to its re-creations of epic characters the conscious poise and spiritual serenity of its masters. The loss of most of the sculpture about which information from antiquity has survived and the silence of this information about those matters with which we here are mainly concerned will require the reader to look upon the surviving evidence as merely the fragments of a once fuller story.

RECORDED VERSIONS OF TROJAN LEGEND.—The cedar chest in which the early Corinthian ruler, Cypselus, as a baby was supposed to have been concealed by his mother for protection later was dedicated in the temple of Hera at Olympia. The Greek traveler Pausanias, whose *Tour in Greece* is still an indispensable handbook for scholarly travelers in Greece, saw this chest and has left us a description of the elaborate scenes wrought upon it in ivory, gold, and cedar. There are scenes, among others, of the Trojan legend: Achilles and Memnon fighting under the direction of their mothers (a subject found elsewhere in the archaic Greek arts); Hector fighting Ajax; and Helen being escorted away from confinement at the hands of Theseus by her brothers Castor and Pollux. There are also Agamemnon; Hermes leading the three goddesses to Paris for judgment; Ajax dragging Cassandra from the image of Athena; and Patroclus dying.[1]

In very recent years a series of sandstone metopes dating shortly before the middle of the sixth century B.C. was found in a Greek sanctuary of Hera near Paestum in southern Italy. These metopes portrayed, among other subjects, scenes from the Trojan cycle featuring Achilles, Troilus, Hector, Patroclus, Hecuba, and Andromache.

In the local museum at Delphi are parts of the frieze which

once adorned the east side of the Treasury of the Siphnians. The frieze portrays a Homeric battle over a fallen warrior in the presence of two groups of seated divinities. On one end of the frieze the fallen warrior Sarpedon is shown being attacked by the Greeks under Menelaus, and on the other, being defended by the Trojans under Hector and Aeneas.

The sculptural pieces, now in Munich, of the two pediments of the local goddess Aphaia's temple at Aegina in all likelihood represent battles of Greeks against Trojans. While these Aeginetan sculptures constitute an important chapter in our knowledge of the history of Greek art, specific details concerning the identity of the several pieces are unknown to us.

Pausanias saw at Olympia, near the temple of Zeus, a sculptural group made by Onatas and dedicated by the Achaeans. It represented the Greek warriors who, accepting Hector's challenge to combat, drew lots to determine who should confront the Trojans. The group of eight or nine statues, among them one of Agamemnon, probably was set on a curved pedestal. Facing this group stood Nestor with the lots in a helmet.[2] At Olympia, also, was another dedicatory offering commemorative of the Trojan War, made by the people of Apollonia on the Ionian Sea. The sculptor was Lycius, the son of Myron. The offering was in the form of a semicircular pedestal upon which stood pairs of heroes who opposed one another in the Trojan War, as follows: at the outer ends of the pedestal Achilles and Memnon, whose mothers, Thetis and Dawn, were represented in the center of the pedestal as supplicating Zeus in behalf of their sons; and, to proceed inwards toward the center from both ends, Odysseus and Helenus, Menelaus, and Paris, Diomedes and Aeneas, and Ajax and Deiphobus.[3] For literary background, a tragedy of Aeschylus called the *Psychostasia* or *The Weighing of Souls* described Thetis and Dawn in heaven as each imploring Zeus to spare the life of her son. The contest between Achilles and Memnon, originally a part of the cyclic epic, *Aethiopis,* Pausanias also saw portrayed in relief on a throne of Apollo at Amyclae. Its maker was Bathycles the Magnesian, who probably flourished in the middle of the sixth century B.C. Another of its reliefs portrayed Hermes leading the three goddesses to Paris for judgment.[4]

Pausanias also saw on the Acropolis at Athens a replica in bronze of the wooden horse of Troy. Its base, bearing the name of Strongylion, who made the figure, has been found on the Acropolis. Pausanias says that Menestheus and Teucer, as well as the sons of Theseus, were peeping out of the horse.[5]

Some of the metopes on the north side of the Parthenon depicted scenes from the sack of Troy.

The reliefs on the frieze of a tomb found at Gyolbashi, the site of ancient Trysa in Lycia, portray, among other mythological stories, the siege of Troy. These reliefs are thought to have been made under the influence of Polygnotus.[6]

The Argive Heraeum, erected anew on a different site by the architect Eupolemus of Argos when the original temple had been destroyed by fire in 423 B.C., was a fitting place for its sculptures, now lost, depicting the Trojan War and the taking of Ilium,[7] for in the ancient Heraeum, according to tradition, the Greek chieftains swore allegiance to Agamemnon before setting out for Troy.

The sculptor Scopas set up in Bithynia a large Achilles ensemble containing statues, among others, of Neptune and Thetis, and of the Nereids and Tritons. The elder Pliny[8] declared it a splendid work and probably it was. This group later was carried to Rome and set up in the Circus Flaminius.

SURVIVING VERSIONS OF THE TROJAN LEGEND.—The museums of Europe and America contain many representations in sculpture of characters who belong to the legend of the

Trojan War. A few of these may be mentioned: the early archaic relief of Agamemnon with his herald Talthybius and Epeus (in the Louvre);[9] the lovely marble relief in Naples of Paris, Eros, Aphrodite, Helen, and Peitho;[10] the marble group supposed to represent Menelaus and the dead Patroclus (in the Loggia dei Lanzi at Florence);[11] the two sarcophagi in the Vatican, with their reliefs of the contest of Achilles and Penthesilea;[12] the statue of Paris holding the apple to be awarded to one of the three goddesses (who may originally have formed a group with him) and the well-known Laocoön group,[13] both in the Vatican; the Trojan Tablet and the beautiful reliefs on a sarcophagus depicting episodes in the career of Achilles, both in the Capitoline Museum in Rome. The famous Portland Vase in the British Museum contained the ashes belonging to this sarcophagus. One of the scenes on the sarcophagus depicts Priam kneeling before Achilles in supplication for the body of his son.[14] There is also a Graeco-Roman relief of the death of Priam in the Boston Museum of Fine Arts.[15] On the relief in Naples recently mentioned Paris is constrained by Eros, the winged god of love, while Aphrodite with motherly tenderness reassured the passive and reflective Helen. Peitho, the goddess of Persuasion, sat above Helen.

The Laocoön group, consisting of that Trojan priest and his two sons being strangled by serpents, once adorned the palace of Titus, who was the Roman emperor during the years 79-81 A.D., and in whose reign the Coliseum was dedicated. A work of the first century B.C., this group was highly praised by the Elder Pliny,[16] who attributes it to the three Rhodian sculptors, Agesander and his sons, Polydorus and Athenodorus. Its accidental discovery, in January 1506, in the historic ground successively occupied by the residence of Maecenas, the Golden House of Nero, and the baths of Titus brought considerable excitement to the humanistic court of Julius II.

The Trojan Horse. Glass paste.
Formerly in private collection, Rome. See page 149

Bernini. *Aeneas, Anchises, Ascanius.*
Borghese Museum, Rome. See page 157

Michelangelo was one of the first to reach the spot after its discovery. The man who discovered the group under his vine-yard was rewarded with a grant of the taxes of the S. Giovanni Gate for the remaining years of his life. The eighteenth century went into rapturous excesses over it, calling it a silent poem and the Homer of art. Byron's description of the group[17] testifies to the warm admiration felt for it in his day, too. Its vogue has passed since the recovery and appreciation of earlier Greek originals at Athens and elsewhere.

The Trojan Tablet (*tabula Iliaca*) discussed in the third chapter is a marble tablet ten inches high and eleven and a half inches wide, with many details of the Trojan legend and in-scriptions pertaining thereto cut on it in low relief. It is one of what originally formed a number of such tablets used in schools for instructional purposes, to which latter fact an inscription on it testifies. The tablet has on it a portrayal of events of the *Iliad*, of the *Aethiopis* of Arctinus, of the *Little Iliad* of Lesches, and of the *Sack of Troy* by Stesichorus. The *Sack of Troy* occupied the central portion, between two pillars (the left one is missing). On the top of the tablet are scenes from the first book of the *Iliad*. Scenes from the other books once ran down both sides, though those on the left are lost. Inscriptions accompany all the scenes, and a summary of the *Iliad* in prose is cut upon the pillar remaining. The base which supports the pillars contains a series of scenes from the *Aethiopis* and *Little Iliad*, among them being the following: Achilles slaying Penthesilea, Thersites, and Memnon; the battle around the corpse of Achilles, and his burial; the contest for the arms of Achilles; the theft of the Palladium; and the entry of the wooden horse into the city.

In the Bibliothèque Nationale in Paris there is a marble fragment of another *tabula Iliaca* in which Priam falls to his knees before Achilles at the door of Achilles' tent, begging him to release the body of his son. The wagon bearing the ransom is behind Priam.[18]

There are several busts of Homer in existence, as, for example, that in Munich and that in Boston. The latter is thought to be one of several coming from a Hellenistic original.[19] The idealized portrait of the blind bard in the National Museum of Naples, which is reproduced in the frontispiece of this book, is thought to be one of the best. In the British Museum in London there is a tablet portraying in relief the apotheosis of Homer.[20] In the upper part of it are found Jupiter, Apollo, and the nine Muses on a cavernous hill. At the bottom of the relief Homer is enthroned between the kneeling figures of the *Iliad* and the *Odyssey*. He is attended by such personifications as Time and the World, History, Myth, Poetry, Tragedy, and Comedy. And in a group to his right are Nature, Virtue, Memory, Faith, and Wisdom. The relief is inscribed with the name of the sculptor Archelaos and probably is a work of the third century B.C. One thinks of the painting by Ingres depicting the same subject and similarly prompted by a devotion to Homer. This and little else the periods of the two artists had in common.

## ANCIENT GEMS

EXTENT, USES, HISTORY.—One of the minor artistic attainments of the Greeks, Etruscans, and Romans, which prevailed from prehistoric Greek times to late Roman times, not to mention its recurrence in the Renaissance and in succeeding centuries to the present, was the engraving of gems. Since, naturally, the art did not develop in a vacuum, it was affected by other contemporary skills of the respective periods, and, of course, the developing of the skill of engraving gems can not be divorced from the history of the respective periods nor from the levels of artistic skills in those periods. Gems in

146

countless numbers and of every conceivable stage of value and skill were made by the Greeks, the Etruscans, and the Romans. Recovered from the wreckage of the ancient world, large and important collections of gems exist in a score of places in the Western World. Gems were used by the ancients as works of art in and of themselves, as seals, as amulets with supposed curative and protective powers, and as ornaments for use on personal apparel, couches, tripods, household utensils, garlands, arms, and musical instruments.

The most common subjects engraved on gems were from mythology and daily living. The aged art of engraving gems, revived in the sixth century B.C., reached its highest level in Greece in the fifth and fourth centuries B.C. The highly creative epoch of the second half of the fifth century B.C. in Greece found expression in this minor art as well as in the major fine arts. One can see in the engraved gems of this period, subject, of course, to the limitations attending miniature artistic work in the expression of emotions and spiritual qualities, something of that same beauty and grace of proportion and design and of that same serenity which are an obvious feature of the major arts. Unfortunately, however, comparatively few Greek gems of this period have survived.

The Etruscans from the end of the sixth to the end of the fourth centuries B.C. carried on in Italy extensive work in the engraving of gems. Some of their finest work was done in the first half of the fifth century. While their work shows great technical skill and finish and often cannot be distinguished from Greek work, it lacked imagination and originality and relied considerably for motivation on Greek patterns and legends, mostly Homeric and Theban. Roman gems came into their happiest period in the first century after Christ, but the artists who made them were Greek.

TROJAN LEGEND ON GEMS.—The various episodes of the

Trojan legend provided the engravers of gems with a constant source of material for their skills. A Graeco-Roman (i.e., of the Roman Empire) imitation of an amethyst (in the British Museum) bears an impression of the familiar story of the judgment of Paris. Seated on a rock under a tree and attended by his flock Paris is accosted by Hermes, behind whom come Athena, Hera, and Aphrodite.[21] Other versions of this legend are on other gems of classical origin, such as the sardonyx cameo in Berlin,[22] and even on gems of postclassical times.[23]

The events of Achilles' career at Troy are particularly common on gems. He may be seen seizing by the hair the young Troilus, who is mounted on a galloping horse;[24] sulking in the seclusion of his tent; playing his lyre; donning his armor; dragging the corpse of Hector behind his chariot; supporting the vanquished Penthesilea, an especially common theme; and suffering from his wound. He may also be found in the presence of his mother Thetis, of Ajax and Odysseus, of Priam, and at the grave of Patroclus. An Etruscan banded agate scarab belonging perhaps to the middle of the fifth century B.C. shows Achilles wounded in the heel by an arrow.[25] A carnelian ring-stone (in the Metropolitan Museum) of the period of the Roman Republic shows Ajax carrying the dead Achilles, who has an arrow in his left foot. Both heroes wear helmets and cuirasses, and on the ground lies a shield. This part of Achilles' career is a recurring subject both on gems and Greek vases.[26]

Other well-known characters of the *Iliad* appear on gems, too. The parting scene of Hector from his wife and child might well be expected to occur, and it does. On a black paste gem in Berlin the small Astyanax reaches out his little hand to his father from the arms of his mother, while Hector gazes upon her before departing for battle.[27] A sardonyx, also in Berlin, shows Hector stretching out his hands to his child, whom Andromache holds out to him for the last greeting of his father.[28] The rendezvous of Dolon with death at the hands of Odysseus and Diomedes is found engraved on one gem at least, and possibly two, in the British Museum;[29] and on another, Menelaus supports the body of Patroclus.[30] Then there are (on a gem in Florence) Teucer and Ajax in the battle at the ships,[31] and Hector setting fire to a Greek ship.[32]

The details of the sack of Troy provide the subjects of a large number of engraved gems. An Etruscan carnelian scarab in the Metropolitan Museum of Art in New York bears a representation of the Trojan horse, out of which the Greeks clamber in the dead of night by the light of a small crescent moon.[33] A fragmentary glass paste of the Augustan period has on it an engraving of the Trojan horse; in the background are a tower and the walls of the acropolis; on the battlement a woman, possibly Cassandra, shrieks and holds her arms outstretched. In the foreground the huge wooden horse stands on rollers. Six Greek warriors have emerged through a door in the side of the horse, and they reach the ground by rope and ladder.[34] In the British Museum a carnelian scarab of Etruscan workmanship belonging to the end of the fifth century B.C. shows Laocoön and his two sons being attacked by three serpents.[35] Numerous other representations of the Laocoön story extend into the Renaissance.[36]

Among other scenes attendant upon the sack of Troy the seizure of Cassandra is often found engraved upon gems. On a Graeco-Roman gem in the British Museum is a portrayal of Ajax seizing Cassandra by the hair as she sits on an altar embracing the Palladium.[37] The legend had been known at Rome and used on gems for a long time prior to this, and it may also be found on a ringstone in the late postclassical period.[38] The pathos of Polyxena's sad fate is expressed by the gem engraver as well as by other artists. A paste imitation of a sard in the British Museum shows Neoptolemus with sword raised in his right hand about to slay Polyxena, who kneels before him with head bent.[39] The suicide of Ajax, son of Telamon, is also a recurring theme, as several gems in the British Museum and elsewhere testify. Nor was the escape of Aeneas from Troy with father and son passed over unobserved by the gem engravers. Though the details vary, the story became virtually canonized. On a carefully executed Etruscan carnelian scarab in Paris a youthful Aeneas, his right knee on the ground and shield on his left arm, is represented as carrying Anchises on his left shoulder. Anchises bears the family sacraments in his hand.[40] This gem long antedates any distinctly Roman interest in the legend of Aeneas. On an engraved gem of the Hellenistic period in Berlin, a gem of brown-black glass paste, Aeneas may be seen kneeling to take up Anchises, while Ascanius goes ahead.[41] On a carnelian of the late Republican period (in Berlin) is the familiar and common scene, especially on post-Vergilian gems, of Aeneas carrying Anchises, with the customary sacraments in a chest, and Ascanius being led by the hand of Aeneas.[42] The British Museum has at least three versions of this subject in its gem collection.[43]

## ANCIENT COINS

NATURE OF SKILL AND EXTENT OF ITS PRODUCTS.—In the ancient world the striking of coins, like the engraving of gems, which is by nature closely related to it, is another art which generally rings true to the artistic standards and reflects the historical development and economic history of the several respective periods of ancient civilization. The coin—that "pale and common drudge 'tween man and man"—must of necessity be close to the realities of life. Above all other artistic creations it reaches the common man in his daily life and thoughts. The message of the coin, whatever it may be, is sure to become part of the popular consciousness. As an added token of genuineness, the coin, like the inscription, generally comes to us untampered with and unrestored by later hands. Greek and Roman coins of innumerable municipalities over a period of more than a thousand years have come down to us in great numbers, and form important collections in museums all over the Western World. Probably the most important collections are in London, Berlin, Paris, and Vienna.[44]

HISTORY.—The history of Greek coinage covers a period of a thousand years, beginning with the seventh century B.C. By the middle of the sixth century the issuance of coinage was widely prevalent all over the Eastern Mediterranean. By the time of the Persian Wars most of the important places in the Greek world, including southern Italy and Sicily, had their own coinage. Few of these coins, however, enjoyed a wide circulation or recognition. From the time of the Persian Wars the silver owls of Athens won a growing prestige and became common currency abroad, just as the Roman currency of the Empire enjoyed universal circulation and respect. The flourishing period of Greek coinage corresponds with the existence of free cities in Greece in the century and a half between the expulsion of the Persians (480 B.C.) and the accession of Alexander (332 B.C.). The skill of the Greek sculptor may be seen in the small on the Greek coins of the best period, with due allowance for the limitations inherent in such small space; but unfortunately the coinage of Athens, with all its prestige abroad, did not keep pace with her otherwise high standards of artistic achievement.

Famous statues, like the statue of Athena made by Phidias for the Parthenon at Athens and his statue of Zeus at Olympia, were reproduced on coins. Coins were of silver (which became the customary metal for coins in Greece) and of electrum, gold, and bronze.

151

Etruscan coinage began about 500 B.C. Roman coinage was first struck at about the middle of the fourth century B.C., and continued until the fall of the Western Empire in the late fifth century of our era. Probably the best and purest period of Roman coinage in terms of artistic excellence was that of Augustus. Coins of the Roman Empire are at least not below the standards of excellence of the contemporary sculpture. The usual Roman coinage was of bronze and silver, though gold and brass were used occasionally.

SUBJECTS OF ENGRAVINGS.—Throughout the history of ancient coinage, legendary heroes, founders, patron deities, and demigods are honored with places on coins. In Greek times the number of such types or representations is virtually coextensive with the legends, heroes, and patron deities of the city-states which honeycombed the Mediterranean area from Spain to the inner reaches of Asia Minor. On Roman coins, too, early and late, legendary characters continued to be used to commemorate an early tradition and to indoctrinate the populace with an idea or a tradition. And so various parts of the Trojan legend perpetuated themselves in the minds of the rank and file of the people of the ancient world through coins as they could through no other medium, insofar, at least as the ancients actually observed what was engraved on the coins for which they toiled.

The flight of Aeneas from Troy is a commonly recurring subject on coins, from early Greek to late Roman times. A silver four-drachma piece of Aenea on the Thermaic Gulf in Macedonia — a town which Aeneas was thought to have founded—is said to be the earliest of the surviving representations of a Trojan myth in the history of coinage. A coin of the sixth century B.C., it depicts Aeneas carrying Anchises. He is preceded by his wife Creusa, who carries Ascanius.[45] As we know from surviving specimens,[46] Aeneas appears also on other coins of this town, silver and bronze, during the fifth and fourth centuries B.C. A bronze coin of the Sicilian town of Segesta bearing a representation of Aeneas carrying Anchises[47] emphasizes the value of early legends as a force in the cementing of international relations, for Segesta, under Roman control after the close of the first Punic War in 241 B.C., claimed relationship to the Romans on the ground of a traditional Trojan descent. Cicero records the belief of the people of the town that Aeneas after his flight from Troy had founded it.[48] The British Museum has two bronze coins of Segesta engraved with the images of Aeneas and his father.[49] One of these coins, of the time of Augustus, shows Aeneas carrying the Palladium and his father. Above the head of Aeneas is a crescent and behind him an eagle with open wings. Coins struck by Julius Caesar about 48 B.C. show the emphasis which he placed upon his supposed ancestral connection with Venus and Aeneas. Five silver *denarii* in the British Museum have on their obverse a head of Venus diademed and on the reverse Aeneas with the Palladium and his father and the name "Caesar."[50] Octavian, too, prior to his undisputed accession to power, issued around 39 B.C. an *aureus* with his head on the face of the coin and on its reverse Aeneas carrying his father.[51]

That both political expediency and pride in local tradition perpetuated the legend of Aeneas' piety throughout the Empire is evident from the abundance of extant coins of this type. To the reading world Vergil reinterpreted the story in unforgettable narrative. But coinage gave Augustus a still wider medium through which he might disseminate throughout the Empire an illusion of piety and tradition about himself. And yet in the early imperial period the legend did not assume the place in coinage which it had either in the late Republic or in the later imperial period. A dominant feature of the character of Trajan, whose reign fell in the early second century of our era, was his interest in bringing the military glory of Rome into sharp focus. To this end he used the coinage of the Empire by reissuing, probably in the year A.D. 107, on *aurei* and *denarii* some of the obsolete republican types of historic interest. A coin of this type is the revival of the silver *denarius* mentioned above as issued by Caesar about the year 48 B.C.[52] The benign Antoninus Pius of the middle of the second century also strove to indoctrinate his people with a reverence for the fine traditions of Rome's past. His coinage testifies to this, particularly in its adoption of Aeneas' pious devotion to father and son as a heroic model. There survive from the mint of Rome from his reign an *aureus* depicting Aeneas in military dress carrying Anchises, who holds a box of sacraments, and leading Ascanius by the hand;[53] and also brass *sestertii* and bronze coins of similar type.[54]

Roman towns in the Troad by issuing commemorative coins made capital of the tradition which linked them with the early beginnings of Rome through Aeneas. Thus one of the types found on the coins of Ilium during the Empire is the flight of Aeneas. In the reign of Augustus, Ilium issued a bronze coin portraying Aeneas carrying Anchises.[55] Another bronze coin of Ilium of the second century bears a bust of Athena on the face and on the reverse Aeneas in armor leading Ascanius and carrying Anchises.[56] This group appears commonly on the coins of Ilium. The British Museum has bronze coins of similar type from Dardanus in the reign of Geta,[57] and also from the town of Scepsis, under the name of Julia Mamaea.[58] Old Scepsis was thought to have been founded by the family of Aeneas. This type, however, was not restricted to any one reign in any of the towns of the Troad.

The piety of Aeneas was commemorated on coins of widely distant parts of the Empire. The usual portrayal is the familiar grouping of Aeneas with father and son. Coins paying honor to Aeneas have survived from Laodiceia in Phrygia,[59] Apameia in Bithynia,[60] Otrus in central Phrygia,[61] Patras on the mainland of Greece,[62] and Beirut in Phoenicia.[63]

The judgment of Paris is also depicted on Roman coins of Ilium and Scepsis, of Tarsus in Cilicia, and of Alexandria in Egypt.[64] A bronze coin of the late Empire from Tarsus represents Paris seated on a rock with an apple in his right hand and a crook in his left. Before him stands the nude Aphrodite with both hands raised to her hair. She is followed by Hera and Athena.[65]

Hector, too, was honored often on the coinage of Ilium during the Empire. He had a temple and a statue in historical Ilium and was thought by the Ilians to haunt their city and the plains. Ilium had no political importance until the time of Alexander the Great. Also, under the Roman Republic it received little or no honor for its historic past, and much damage. But the Empire brought it due recognition. The British Museum has coins of Ilium issued in the reigns of most of the Roman emperors from Augustus to Gordian III. Hector is represented on some as an armed warrior and champion of his country.[66] On a coin of the reign of Caracalla, Hector advances with a shield in his left hand and with right hand raised hurling a torch or spear at two ships in which rowers may be seen.[67] On a bronze coin of the reign of Commodus he stands armed in a *quadriga* or four-horse chariot.[68] On a bronze coin of the reign of Septimius Severus he is in full armor with his left foot on the prostrate body of Patroclus, from which he draws a spear. On his left arm he has a shield, and in the field of the coin is the shield of Patroclus.[69] Since there was a grave dedicated to Hector in the town of Ophrynium in the Troad, it has been assumed that a warrior depicted on many of the town's coins is Hector.

Athena, too, is honored often—and justly so—on the coinage

of Ilium, both early and late.[70] And the memory of Homer was kept alive on coins of many ages and places, including Ios, Amastris, Nicaea, Cyme, Temnus, Colophon, Smyrna, and Chios. He is sometimes represented as seated, with a scroll of his works on his lap.[71] The abduction of Ganymede by the eagle of Zeus is found on coins of both Ilium and Dardanus. One such bronze imperial coin has on its face a bust of a turreted female representing Rome.[72] Other characters of the Trojan legend found on ancient coins are Priam, Helen, Protesilaus, Diomedes, Achilles, Ajax, the Scamander River, Hephaestus, and Thetis.

## MODERN SCULPTURE

RENAISSANCE.—In the centuries intervening since antiquity, sculpture has been put to many uses. Since classical mythology has been one of these, Trojan subjects have had their due place. It should be said in all candor, however, that other phases of classical mythology, especially those which lent themselves readily to allegorical or symbolical interpretation, have sought expression in marble more insistently. And much of the sculpture of the Renaissance, upon which the classical influence was dominant, went into the elaborate religious and secular projects of the time. The era of Renaissance sculpture may be thought to begin during the period 1410-1430. The cultural flow in and from Italy across the face of Europe as outlined in previous chapters may be assumed also for sculpture.

SPREADING INTEREST IN CLASSICAL ART IN EIGHTEENTH CENTURY.—The eighteenth century witnessed a growing wave of new contacts of Europe with classical Rome and Greece through travel, study of surviving monuments, and new discoveries. Etruria, Herculaneum, and Pompeii became important centers of new discoveries, and knowledge of these spread quickly throughout Europe. Excavations were begun at Herculaneum in 1738 and at Pompeii in 1748. After the middle of the century travel to Greece ceased to be a venture into the unknown, and in the last quarter of that century travel literature regarding Greece and serious studies of Greek art were abundant even in England, which was late in coming under the spell of the classical revival.

Newly found monuments of the classical heritage brought forth a new body of esthetic criticism which deeply affected contemporary artists and their works. The greatest name in the history of artistic criticism in the period is that of Winckelmann, whose *Geschichte der Kunst des Alterthums* (1764) is a landmark in the history of criticism of ancient art. Winckelmann had never visited Greece nor seen at first hand even the Greek sculpture which was known at that time; yet on the basis of the evidence available to him he brought into clear focus the qualities of simplicity, serenity, and nobility inherent in Greek art, though at times seeing these qualities in works of art where they do not exist to any marked degree. Winckelmann's worshiping conception of Greek art found wide acceptance first in Germany, then throughout Europe and England, before the century was out. One of the bases of the romantic attitude toward all things Greek, prevalent in the nineteenth century, lay in his work. Under the stimulus of the newly discovered antiquities of Italy and of newly discovered Greece, societies were formed in various countries of Europe, and especially in England, whose purpose it was to foster the study of classical antiquity and impart an acquaintance with Italy and Greece.

BERNINI, CANOVA.—The two leading spirits in the renewed admiration of Roman antiquity were Bernini (1598-1680) and Canova (1757-1822). The well-known group of Aeneas, Anchises, and Ascanius, made by Bernini, who was the architect of the colonnade of St. Peter's, and a roving apostle of international good will, is in the Museum of the Villa Borghese in Rome. This group was made by the artist while he was still in early manhood. It is a work of great technical skill, though there is felt sometimes in the faces a lack of strength and heroism, which may derive in part from the model of Bernini for this work (Michelangelo's *Christ* in Santa Maria sopra Minerva in Rome). Typically enough, Roman legend and the genius of Michelangelo helped Bernini to maturity of skill.

Canova made three bas-reliefs in illustration of the Trojan story: *The Death of Priam, Briseis Consigned to the Heralds by Patroclus,* and *The Offering of the Trojan Matrons.*[73] Canova's rendering of the death of Priam follows the Vergilian account. In the court of Priam's palace Hecuba and her daughters in despair and panic supplicate the gods for help. Priam's young son Polites lies prostrate on the ground. Neoptolemus, having seized Priam by the hair, has dragged him to the altar and is about to slay him with a dagger. Hecuba faints into the arms of an attendant maid. Being an Italian, Canova was, naturally, closer to the Latin than to the Greek tradition. His relief of Briseis being led away from Achilles (1794) should be considered in comparison with renderings of the same subject by Flaxman (1793) and Thorvaldsen (1804). After Canova's death two semi-colossal statues were found in his studio in an unfinished condition. The artist had begun them many years before. The scene they represented, the combat of Hector and Ajax, may be found in the seventh book of the *Iliad*. His Hector stands with drawn sword awaiting the attack of the foe, while the fierce Ajax is on the point of drawing his sword from his scabbard.[74] Canova's bust of Helen is best known through Byron's verses about it.[75] Canova also made a statue of Paris, which is in Munich.

NEOCLASSICISM IN BRITAIN.—The history of neoclassicism in Britain will be briefly told. The medium through which it found expression, naturally enough in view of the nature of the discoveries in Italy, was sculpture. No significant work in painting had gone on in England since the fifteenth century except in the field of miniature, and most of the mediocre painters were foreigners. Among those who brought to England from Rome an enthusiastic devotion to ancient art were William Palmer, Peter Scheemaker, and Thomas Banks. The latter (1735-1805) made a colossal statue of Achilles mourning the loss of Briseis. Until the middle of the eighteenth century sculptural work in England was almost wholly funerary. After that time its uses were more diversified. In the early years of the Academy concentration upon the ancient and complete scorn for what was not in keeping with its spirit were practiced and officially sanctioned. The portrayal of modern dress upon a statue was regarded as a degradation of the art of sculpture. Realism in characterization was abandoned in favor of idealized generalization. A statue of Dr. Johnson in St. Paul's has been taken to represent people as diverse as St. Paul himself and a retired gladiator meditating upon a wasted life. Great emphasis was laid upon the human form, and a sculptor was advised to know as much anatomy as a surgeon. Statues were at first made in the nude, but the obviously unesthetic nature of certain subjects and the effect of certain results led to the compromise of draping figures in togas. The artificiality and unreality of this excessive zeal to embalm the present in the past were swept away with the coming of the French Revolution and the Romantic movement.

THORVALDSEN.—The Dane, Thorvaldsen (1770-1844) was also an ardent neoclassicist. He ascribed the date of his birth to the day of his first arrival in Rome, where Canova was at the height of his popularity, and he spent most of his life there. The effect of ancient statuary on him was as profound as his study of it was thorough. Nor could he be expected to remain untouched by the wave of philhellenism which swept over northern Europe from the end of the eighteenth century. Though entirely ignorant of Greek he was deeply impressed by the beauty of Homer and delighted in the legends of Greece.

In the spring of 1805 he finished his first significant bas-relief in marble, *The Abduction of Briseis,* which is still regarded as one of his greatest works. It is now in Mitau, Russia. In this relief, Briseis, delivered to the heralds of Agamemnon by Patroclus, sadly leaves Achilles, who turns his head away in violent anger. It is a memorable scene in Homer, of fine restraint, and it has well deserved the many re-creations of it which it has had in the arts. Both Flaxman and Canova had previously handled the story.

Another marble bas-relief of Homeric origin among the works of Thorvaldsen is his *Hector and Paris.* Its source lies in that part of the sixth book of the *Iliad* where Hector chides Paris for lingering in the palace with Helen while disaster hovers close on the battlefield outside. In the relief, Helen, who is busily engaged, raises her eyes toward Hector. In a later copy of this relief the sculptor went beyond Homer in having two handmaidens of Helen offer Paris a distaff.[76]

In a marble bas-relief in the Thorvaldsen Museum Achilles dresses the wound of his friend, Patroclus, and in another, *The Arms of Achilles,* Athena gives Odysseus the arms of Achilles as Ajax turns away full of anger and Thetis sits weeping beside the tomb of her son.

Another of Thorvaldsen's bas-reliefs in marble is *The Parting of Hector and Andromache.* It portrays Hector raising Astyanax in his arms and invoking the gods. Andromache leans sadly on her husband's shoulder and Paris advances to join Hector. Thorvaldsen also made both a plaster and a marble bas-relief on the subject of Priam beseeching Achilles for the body of Hector. In the former of the two Achilles

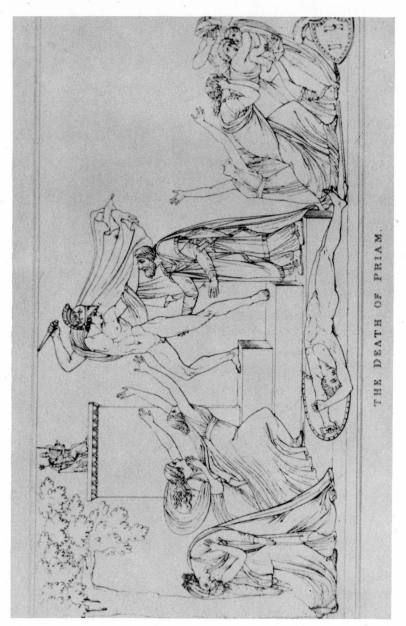

THE DEATH OF PRIAM.

*Canova. The Death of Priam.* See page 158

Thorvaldsen. *The Abduction of Briseis.* Mitau, Russia. See page 160

raises the aged man from the ground, just as he had done in Homer.[77] The pathos of Achilles' belated discovery of Penthesilea's beauty held the fancy of this sculptor for many years. A marble bas-relief in the Thorvaldsen Museum portrays it. Surprised at the beauty of the vanquished queen, Achilles raises her from the ground. It was for Andrew Lang to develop the emotion of the scene in which Achilles, raising the fallen Penthesilea, discovers her beauty.[78]

A plaster bas-relief of Homer in the Thorvaldsen Museum was designed along with some reliefs of Trojan scenes to adorn the pedestal of a statue of Achilles, though the sculptor never made the statue. H. W. Bissen (1798-1868), understudy and collaborator of Thorvaldsen, became the pre-eminent sculptor of Denmark after the death of his master. A work of his is an *Achilles* which shows the Homeric hero in an angry mood.[79]

The Romantic movement laid a gentle hand on Hellenism in these reliefs of Thorvaldsen. The happy wedding of the two forces, as in the writings of the English poets, protected Romanticism from its own excesses and imparted to Hellenism an emotional fullness which the ancients at their best chose not to allow. The achievement of Thorvaldsen in these reliefs lies in his ability to impart to the graceful beauty and serene repose associated with Greek relief an emotional, often feminine, softness, a melancholy wistfulness, a regret that sadness and tragedy must haunt the lives of men and women so fair.

OTHER ARTISTS.—To conclude, the work of some other artists of modern times on the Trojan legend will be mentioned. In the Loggia dei Lanzi at Florence stands the group called *The Rape of Polyxena by Pyrrhus*. It is the work of Pio Fedi (1816-1892). The French artist, Eugène Guillaume (1822-1905) made an *Andromache*. His contemporary and fellow countryman, Jean Carpeaux (1827-1875), like many of his fellow artists, found his real genius through his dozen years of residence at Rome. His representation of Achilles wounded in the heel was attended by honorable mention. He also made a statue *Philoctetes on the Island of Lemnos,* and a short time later won the *prix de Rome* with his statue of Hector bearing his son Astyanax in his arms and imploring the gods for his son's welfare. In the garden of the Villa Achilleion, built for the Empress Elizabeth of Austria, on the beautiful island of Corfu, which is so charmingly portrayed by Homer,[80] was placed a recumbent statue of the wounded or dying Achilles, the work of the German sculptor, Herter, in the year 1884.

The relief called *Homer* made by the English artist Harry Bates (1850-1899) left upon a modern conception a touch of classical grace and beauty. Homer is represented as singing to humanity against a background occupied by the Parthenon, Athena, and the rising sun of art.

In Leipzig is the *Cassandra* of the German, Max Klinger.

The subject chosen for the gold medal competition for students of sculpture in 1899, under the auspices of the Royal Academy in London, was the departure of Aeneas from Troy. Of the eight groups presented in this competition, two attracted notable attention for the manly sentiment and courage implicit in the work.[81] Thus have young sculptors served their apprenticeship on this ancient subject.

Very recently the Cleveland Art Museum has acquired one of the few pieces of sculpture made by the French painter, Pierre Auguste Renoir (1841-1920). A splendid bronze in high relief, done between 1916 and 1918, it portrays with a combination of the skills of painter and sculptor the judgment of Paris, a subject to which the artist had devoted himself as a painter a decade earlier.

Paul Manship has been an outstanding American artist of this century. Trained in the American Academy at Rome, he has proved himself a sympathetic observer of ancient sculptural styles and a highly skilled technician in his adaptations of them. His bronze Briseis[82] interprets a Homeric figure in the style of Greek art of the middle of the fifth century B.C.

And so, amid abundant evidence that the ancient legend and the ancient skills portraying it are still a vitalizing influence for the minds and hands of contemporary artists, young and old, this chapter may close with confident assurance that the legend of Troy will live on.

# VI. THE LEGEND IN OPERA

THROUGH opera the three sister arts of poetry, music, and dance, as in the days of Greek tragedy, were once again brought together, and out of their union arose a brilliantly new artistic form.[1] Ancient legend was, from the early days of opera, a common medium through which opera expressed itself. Opera, based on the monodic style, was born in Florence in the latter years of the sixteenth century, out of a realization of the dramatic inadequacies of polyphony and out of the desire to return to what was thought to be the more simple and chastened Greek use of music as subordinate to the word. The occasion for the creation of the first opera yet extant—the *Euridice* of Peri and Caccini (1600)—was the wedding of Henry IV of France and Maria de' Medici. The poet Rinuccini wrote its libretto. Thus made its humble beginning an art which was to have thousands upon thousands of performances upon the public stages of Europe and America during the following centuries; which was to make artists out of popes, duchesses out of human nightingales, librettists out of cardinals, and plenipotentiaries out of virtuosi; and which was to rouse audiences to hysteria, street brawls, suicide, and revolution. Some sixteen opera houses were opened in Venice alone before the year 1700. There commercial opera began, in 1637. Italian opera triumphed over all rivals in the first half of the eighteenth century, but after 1800 opera flourished all over Europe. Bologna, Rome, Turin, and Naples were other important centers for its early growth. Originally intended for the entertainment of royalty, opera demanded luxurious halls

164

and spectacular pageantry, a tendency which grew with the seventeenth century. It is estimated that there exists some information regarding more than 42,000 operas and operettas. The Schatz Collection of librettos in the Library of Congress at Washington includes about 25,000 titles, and since its purchase a large number of additional early librettos has been added to this collection.

### Place of Legend of Troy in Early Opera

A very brief review of the rôle of the Trojan legend in the history of early opera will show in another way the imaginative force of the ancient legend. In general, few subjects can compete in number with the legends of Troy as inspiration for the early operas. As early as the middle of the sixteenth century Claudio Merulo set to music a tragedy of Lodovico Dolce, *The Trojans* (1566), but the resulting fusion was not an opera in the modern sense of the name. From the middle of the seventeenth century, about fifty operas were performed in Italian, French, German, Bohemian, and English which centered around Achilles. Among these were operas on the wrath of Achilles, Achilles and Patroclus, Achilles and Polyxena, and Achilles in the siege of Troy. An instance of the popularity of the opera is the *Achilles* of Paer, first produced in Italian in Vienna in 1801, and later at Prague, Dresden, Paris, Mannheim, Forli, and Milan; also produced in German at Frankfort, Berlin, St. Petersburg, Budapest, Copenhagen, Prague, and Riga; and in Polish at Warsaw. Agamemnon and Ajax were also the subjects of operas. Over twenty operas pertaining to Andromache were performed in Italian, English, Spanish, and French, and numerous others on Briseis, Cassandra, and Helen. Paris, too, was the subject of a dozen operas, especially his judging of the three goddesses, his early love for Oenone, and his abduction of Helen. Polyxena, too, was a favorite subject.

In the period, 1670-1696, twelve operas on Penelope were given at Vienna, Hamburg, Venice, Palermo, Paris, Naples, Trieste, and Rome. The fortunes of Troy in its hour of siege and fall received abundant treatment, too, being the subject of the following operas: *The Virgin Prophetess* or *The Siege of Troy* with an English libretto of Elkanah Settle set to music by the German Gottfried Finger (*fl.* 1682-1723), musician to James II; *Troia* in German by Georg Schürmann (*c.* 1672-1751); *The Burning of Troy* (1757) in Italian by Pasquale Cafaro (1706-1787); *The Destruction of Troy* (1770) in Italian by Michele Mortellari (1750-1807); and *The Trojan Horse* of Giuseppe Woelff, produced in German in Vienna (1799).[2]

The infant mortality rate for the endless profusion of operas written and performed has been prodigiously high; and one should not assume that in point of either musical or dramatic merit many of them deserved less than death. Whatever the motives of their audiences in attending these operas, it is safe to suppose that they came out of no academic interest in the past, and went away satisfied because they were entertained and acquainted with their own possibilities and the possibilities of human life.

Enough academic information was available to make possible the re-creating of Greek setting and costume for many of the operas, if the author wanted it; but, regardless of setting and costume, the interpretation of the ancient story must have been normally in terms of the contemporary rather than of the ancient. Contemporary costume, however, was felt to detract from the spectacle of the opera. The intellectual and emotional climate of the period of any specific opera would undoubtedly find its own child in the libretto and music. The ancient element in the opera dealing with ancient legend would be superficial, and the contemporary element, organic.

# THE LEGEND IN OPERA

In freedom of interpretation lies the secret of the perennial freshness of the Trojan legend in its appeal to artists. This independence with respect to orthodox classical texts probably will be felt more strongly in the opera than in the other arts already discussed.

A half century after the inception of opera the severe subordination of music to the rôle merely of accompaniment as aimed at by Peri gave way to extreme forms of vocal gymnastics, exhibitionism, and ephemeral sensationalism. Italian audiences would listen to the aria showpieces of their favorite singers, and then devote the intervals between arias to eating, conversing, and card playing. The abundance and spread of operas on the Trojan legend, however, reveal this artistic form as an important carrier of an ancient legend into the cultural life and hearts of all of Europe, and the Trojan legend as an important medium through which the people of Europe became better acquainted with the emotional range of human life within themselves.

## GLUCK, *Paris and Helen*

Gluck (1714-1787) was one of the cosmopolitan artists of his day whose travels made him an international figure. He still clung to the old classical subjects. Faced with the swinging of the operatic pendulum in which drama and music competed for dominant usurpation of the stage, Gluck welded the two into unity. He therefore made an important contribution to opera by bringing its component parts—now grown mature, independent, and usurping—under control. Music under his restraining hand was given its organic rôle of handmaiden to the action of the opera. What it lost in inorganic frills and millinery it gained in simple dignity and direct truthfulness. His operatic success, when achieved, may be judged by an incident which occurred in the première of his *Iphigenia at Aulis,* in

Paris, on April 9, 1774. People in the audience were so transported by the seeming reality of the story that only with difficulty were they restrained from rushing to the stage to rescue the heroine. His *Paris and Helen* (1769), produced in Vienna in the spirit of his ideas of reform and based upon an Italian libretto of Calzabigi, is a story of the wooing of Helen by Paris at Sparta. The convenient absence of Menelaus (to whom Helen is only engaged!) as an actual character left the stage to Helen and Paris and to Venus and Cupid, who smile upon his courtship and help to consummate it. At the end of the opera Paris and Helen leave the shore near Sparta to the strains of the chorus. The opera has little dramatic movement, but in it is Gluck's most passionate love song, *O del mio dolce ardor*. This opera was not well received, but it has been revived in various forms in the present century.[3]

## BERLIOZ, *The Trojans*

The last and greatest opera of Berlioz (1803-1869), *The Trojans*, written and set to music by the composer during the years 1855-1858, was a fitting tribute to his long and ardent devotion to Vergil. In its original form it had two parts, *The Taking of Troy* in two acts and *The Trojans at Carthage* in three. Berlioz did not live to hear the performance of the first part, which was first given in French, in 1891, at Nice; the latter part is now better known, though neither has ever won any great acclaim on the stage.. Both parts, however, have been revived in a half dozen cities of Europe; and in Glasgow, in 1935, the opera was given in English, and for the first time, in entirety. The opening scene of the first part of his opera is laid in the abandoned camp of the Greeks on the plain of Troy. In the background three shepherds play their flutes on the tomb of Achilles. In the foreground the Trojans in festal mood sing and dance. Then follows the discovery of the wooden horse. Cassandra, whose tragic figure dominates the two acts of this part of the opera, prophesies the impending doom of Troy and begs her lover Coroebus to leave the ill-fated city. The ensuing scene introduces a festival on the plains, in which the Trojans celebrate their deliverance from the enemy. Andromache and Astyanax place flowers on an altar and advance to the throne of Priam. Cassandra again utters an ominous warning. When Aeneas informs the Trojan people of the extraordinary death of Laocoön, they decide as an appeasement to Pallas Athena, whose dedicatory offering has been insulted, to bring the horse inside the walls to her temple. Despite the repeated despairing cries of Cassandra with which the act closes, the Trojans carry out this resolve. The dominant tone of the act is one of great tragic grandeur.

The opening scene of the second act represents the apartment of Aeneas in the palace. As Aeneas sleeps through the night, there appears before him the ghost of Hector, familiar to all readers of Vergil. Telling Aeneas what has happened within the city during the night, the ghost urges him to flee with his son and the images of the gods and to found a new empire in Italy. Aeneas departs with some Trojan soldiers who have sought him out, fights bravely for a hopeless cause, and finally escapes. The next scene carries us to the Trojan women lamenting before the altar of Cybele. Cassandra announces that Aeneas and his companions with the gods of their country have reached the sea. She counsels the Trojan women to die rather than to submit to the approaching Greek hordes. As the Greek soldiers enter, true to her counsel Cassandra stabs herself to death with the words "Italy! Italy!" on her lips.

In *The Trojans at Carthage* Berlioz adopted the general march of events as found in Vergil's story. In the prologue of this opera a rhapsodist recites to an orchestral lament the story of Troy's fall and destruction after ten years of unavailing siege on the part of the Greeks, thanks to the pious fraud of the wooden horse and to the unheeded warnings of Cassandra.

For Berlioz, life was hard and fame slow. His music was romantic, spectacular, and aggressive. It attempts both to speak and to paint. If a brush were a musical instrument, Berlioz would have been a painter.

### OFFENBACH, *The Fair Helen*

This opera of Offenbach (1819-1880) was first presented in French, in Paris, in the year 1864. Soon performances followed in Vienna and Berlin. Though it was at first criticized as a desecration of antiquity, yet it had within it moods, sentiments, and music which made Offenbach the idol of Europe. He created a great vogue for light opera, which also took form in Vienna in the works of the Strauss family and in England in the operas of Gilbert and Sullivan. He was a prolific artist, and his music, though not great, was buoyant and witty. His opera on Helen is an excellent and tuneful example of its type —the *opéra bouffe*. The significant feature of this opera was its applicability to the France of its time. Napoleon III as virtual dictator of France wore an uneasy crown. The unrest, the sense of impending doom, the consequent frivolity and feeling of the futility of things pervade the opera. People of high birth felt uneasy in attending it. The decadence of Greece in the opera was the mirror in which France could see herself, and what she saw was far from reassuring.[4] The opera has been reproduced in a dozen languages other than French. Its most recent revival took place in London in 1932.

### GOLDMARK, *The Prisoner of War*

*The Prisoner of War (Die Kriegsgefangene)* of the Hungarian Goldmark (1830-1915) was produced in Vienna in 1899. It was also given in Cologne and Prague, and in Hungarian, at Budapest in the same year. The setting is the tent of Achilles after the death of Hector. Achilles grieves over the loss of Patroclus, whose urn and ashes he has just laid to rest. Thetis and the Nereids attempt to console him. Briseis, sent to Achilles by Agamemnon, covers the body of Hector with earth, the ritual of due burial; and since she secretly loves Achilles, prays to Aphrodite for his love. In the second act Briseis ministers unto Achilles with drink and song. Priam, escorted by Hermes, comes to beg Achilles for the corpse of his son, and Achilles softens under the added appeal of Briseis. Set free by Achilles, Briseis enters to bid him farewell. But no sooner has she gone to the ship awaiting her than Achilles realizes that he loved her. The finest thing in this romantic opera is the duet of passion between the two lovers.

## SAINT-SAËNS, *Helen*

The *Helen* of Saint-Saëns (1835-1921), first produced in 1904, is a French lyrical poem, written and set to music by the composer under the inspiration of Gluck. It was also produced in Italian and German, and was revived in Paris in 1919. Since the setting is in Sparta, the composition need not concern us directly. The Helen is a distracted, confused heroine, knowing the better but following the worse, and presently she calls upon the gods to save her from herself. Venus stands over her, luring her on to sin and its consequences; whereas Pallas Athena on the other hand sets up in the sky as a deterrent a vision of Troy in flames and Priam slain. Helen finally throws scruples to the winds and sails for Troy with her lover.

Though an artist of great versatility and varied skills Saint-Saëns never developed a music of marked personality or individuality. His schooling included Latin and Greek alike. He also wrote an overture for Sarah Bernhardt's production of Racine's *Andromache*. In the interval between the première of Racine's tragedy and Saint-Saëns' overture to it Grétry produced in 1780 a French lyrical tragedy in three acts called *Andromache*. Inspired partly by Racine's play, it was produced about fifty-five times during the life of the composer. Thus it will be seen in passing that Racine's tragedy, first produced in 1667, has itself had a long and independent tradition lasting into the twentieth century.

The first production of the opera *The Egyptian Helen* of Richard Strauss (1864 . . .) was in 1928. The story of the libretto was suggested to its author, Hugo von Hofmannsthal, by the passage of the *Odyssey* in which Telemachus visited the happily reunited Menelaus and Helen. The relationship of the two stories, however, is one of contrast rather than of similarity. Menelaus, bringing Helen home from Troy, is pressed by a desire to slay her, whereas Helen, on the other hand, is anxious to reinstate herself in his affections. Helen is saved by Aithra, a royal sorceress, and their love is renewed through a magic potion. The lovers are transported to an island off Morocco, where they may enjoy their newly acquired bliss. Within five years after its first appearance this opera was produced in German in Vienna, Berlin, New York, Geneva, The Hague, and Strasbourg, in French in Monte Carlo, in Flemish in Antwerp, and in Hungarian in Budapest.

In 1934 George Antheil's *Helen Retires*, written to a libretto of John Erskine, was staged in New York. Neither the music nor the text won any distinction. As in the other arts, many operas play around the fringes of the Trojan legend, but it has been our attempted policy not to wander too far afield from Troy itself, at least in all directions.

In opera the legend of Troy had a supreme opportunity to touch directly and vividly the life of Europe. The close association of the legend with music and the stage gave to the legend the strength of those authentic expressions of the human spirit in their spectacular development from the early days of opera. And, in turn, the legend of Troy had within itself an accumulated tradition of varied and significant experience which could excite, delight, guide, inspire, and instruct both performers and audience. The expression of the legend on the stage and in entirely new musical achievements insured its freshness; and, on the other hand, by virtue of its origin in a civilization for which Europe was to have a growing admiration, the legend gave Europe a chance to see its own petty adventures, wars, romances, joys, and sufferings magnified to the proportions of epic, lyric, and drama. The contemporary skills of Europe in any one period, through association with the universality which had become the permanent glory of the legend of Troy, strove toward universality themselves. It is likely that opera in Europe reached more people more directly and in more vulnerable moods than any of the other arts. And the disruptive forces at work within European society were such that Europe needed the humanizing pity, fear, and creative enthusiasms which the legend of Troy in operatic form brought to it.

# EPILOGUE

THE LEGEND OF TROY began with Homer, whose poems are still a true measure of human capacities. Since Homer, the legend has lived in its own right as he left it, and it has lived, too, in the language, costume, religion, nationality, and *mores* of many peoples widely separated in time, space, and folkways.

Always the expression of the legend in the various arts has had some part, and often a major part, in the artistic history of a period. Because it has had to bear the great burden of the skills and philosophies of distinguished artists, it has often enabled a period to discover in it what we now think of as the very essence of greatness of that period, and thereby has stimulated artists of later periods to admire and retell and emulate the story by means of the skills and philosophies individual to them.

The expression of the legend through the ages is a miniature kaleidoscopic picture of the history of the West, the ebb and flow of its cultural life, of its successes, failures, potentialities, and limitations. It has been the bearer of a growing sense of universal kinship among men. Without the many succeeding legends of Troy in their many forms, universality itself would be less aware of its own existence and function.

The legend gives meaning and continuity to the diversity of the past. The modern world inherits the legend as a precious legacy, and can find in the legend the artistic and humanistic possibilities of the legend as a basis for further progress. In contrast with the force at large in the modern world which tends to alienate man from man the story of Troy can make man everywhere aware of kinship with men, of many lands and many tongues, both past and present. After all, the balance of these two forces spells war or peace for any generation.

# NOTES

## Notes to Chapter II

1. *Don Juan* 3.23.

2. *Childe Harold's Pilgrimage* 4.5.

3. For an interesting discussion of morality in Homer cf. L. A. Post, "The Moral Pattern in Homer," *Transactions American Philological Association*, LXX (1939) 158-190.

4. For a highly instructive discussion of the significance of Homer in the history of Greek culture see Werner Jaeger *Paideia: the Ideals of Greek Culture* (New York, Oxford University Press, 1939) 34-54.

5. 2.819-823.

6. *Iliad* 13.460f.

7. *Ibid.* 20.179-181.

8. 20.300-308.

9. *Iliad* 3.205-207.

10. *Ibid.* 7.347-353.

11. *Odyssey* 4.242-264.

12. *Ibid.* 4.271-289. This story is later expanded by Tryphiodorus 463-490.

13. *Ibid.* 8.492-520.

14. *Ibid.* 11.523-537.

15. The surviving fragments of these poems and the testimony regarding them may be found in the edition of Homer by D. B. Munro and T. W. Allen (Oxford, Clarendon Press), V (third edition, 1919). A well-documented study of the tradition of Troy's fall in ancient literature is that of Lois W. Brock *The Sack of Troy in Greek and Roman Literature from Homer to Vergil*, a thesis submitted for the Master's degree at Western Reserve University (1938). The initial appearance of each item of the legend is indicated in this dissertation.

16. 2.234-249.

17. According to Apollodorus and Tryphiodorus the signal was given, perhaps by way of poetic justice, by the tomb of Achilles.

18. 8.517f.

19. *Odyssey* 4.502-511.

20. *Aeneid* 1.39-45.

## Notes to Chapter III

1. *Institutiones Oratoriae* 10.1.62.

2. Cf. C.M. Bowra *Greek Lyric Poetry from Alcman to Simonides* (Oxford, Clarendon Press, 1936) 120-125.

3. *Ibid.* 103-106. Also cf. below, 28.

4. See p. 28.

5. J. M. Edmonds *Lyra Graeca* (London, Heinemann, Loeb Classical Library) I (1934) 208f.

6. *Ibid.* 210f.

7. *Ibid.* 226-231.

8. *Ibid.* 392-395.

9. *Ibid.* II (1924) 114-119. Cf. also Bowra, *op. cit.* (see note 2) 262f., 278.

10. Cf. *Isthmian* 8.49-55; *Olympian* 8.31-46; *Paean* 6.

11. Edmonds, *op. cit.* (see note 5) III (1927) 92-95.

12. *Ibid.* 120f.

13. *Pythian* 1.52-55, translation of Sandys *The Odes of Pindar* (London, Heinemann, Loeb Classical Library, 1919) 161.

14. Edmonds, *op. cit.* (see note 11) 188-193.

15. Cf. A. C. Pearson *The Fragments of Sophocles* (Cambridge, University Press, 1917) I xxxi.

16. Aristotle *Poetics* 3.1448a26; Athenaeus 7.277e; Pearson xxiiif.

17. *The Giaour.*

18. Strabo 13.1.53.

19. Cf. Pearson, *op. cit.* (see note 15) II fragment 373.

20. Dionysius of Halicarnassus 1.48.2.

21. 511-567.

22. *Aeneid* 3.39-57.

23. *Ibid.* 3.294-355.

24. *History* 2.113-120.

25. 1.46-48.

26. 340-343.

27. Dionysius 1.48.3.

28. 1226-1280.

29. Servius, *Aeneid* 2.636.

30. The surviving fragments of these authors may be found in Aemilius Baehrens *Fragmenta Poetarum Romanorum* (Leipzig, Teubner, 1886); Otto Ribbeck *Tragicorum Romanorum Fragmenta* (Leipzig, Teubner, 1897); and E. H. Warmington *Remains of Old Latin* (Cambridge, Harvard University Press, Loeb Classical Library, 4 v., 1935-1940).

31. Cf. Baehrens, fragments 4, 5, and 24 (pp. 44, 46); Warmington II 48.5-7, 48.8-10, 54.19-20.

32. Warmington I 8.15, 10.21-23.

33. Vergil's account of the fall of Troy is discussed in H. W. Prescott *The Development of Virgil's Art* (Chicago, University of Chicago Press, 1927), chapter v.

34. Cf. E. Groag and A. Stein *Prosopographia Imperii Romani* (Berlin, De Gruyter, 1933) I 346f.

35. 30-34.

36. Quintus is edited in the Loeb Classical Library (London, Heinemann, 1913) by A. S. Way. For reference to edition of Tryphiodorus and Colluthus see note 39.

37. In his sympathetic study of the Latin literature of the West from the Antonines to Constantine in *The Cambridge Ancient History* (XII 571-610) Professor Rand points out the fact (p. 571) that there was but one political unit at the time—the Roman Empire—and but one literature—Roman literature— written partly in Latin and partly in Greek.

38. *Odyssey* 11.524f.

39. There is an edition of Tryphiodorus (and of Colluthus in the same volume) in the Loeb Classical Library (London, Heinemann, 1928) edited by A. W. Mair.

40. The word is of Greek derivation, meaning "journal." Cf. our word "ephemeral."

41. Cf. J. U. Powell *New Chapters in the History of Greek Literature* (Oxford, Clarendon Press, 1933, third series) 224.

42. *Iliad* 5.9f.

43. *Varia Historia* 11.2. For a translation of the Latin text of Dares see Margaret Schlauch *Medieval Narrative* (N. Y., Prentice-Hall, 1928).

44. Cf. E. B. Atwood "The *Excidium Troie* and Medieval Troy Literature," *Modern Philology* XXXV (1937) 115-128.

45. 4.18.

46. The understanding regarding the use of the Trojan horse has varied. Pausanias says in effect (1.23.8) that anyone who is not an utter fool knows that the wooden horse was a machine for destroying the wall of Troy. For an interpretation of the Trojan horse as a magical palliative cf. W. F. J. Knight *Vergil's Troy* (Oxford, Blackwell, 1932) 112-122.

47. The details of this account of Dictys will be found in the last paragraph of the fourth book and in the fifth book of the text of that author.

48. Bruno Krusch *Scriptores Rerum Merovingicarum* II (in *Monumenta Germaniae Historica,* Hanover, 1888) 45.18, 46.4-9, 93.1-12.

49. *Ibid.* 199.25.

50. *Ibid.* 241-243 (paragraphs 1-2).

51. Cf. Eva Matthews Sanford "The Study of Ancient History in the Middle Ages," *Journal of the History of Ideas* V (1944) 36f.

52. Cf. L. Petit de Julleville *Histoire de la Langue et de la Littérature française* (Paris, Armand Colin, 1910) I 188-220 for an account and appraisal of this work.

53. For a summary of the events attending the fall of Troy in the *Roman de Troie* cf. Petit de Julleville, 194f.

54. In having Antenor settle here Benoit misunderstood the text of Dictys, who says (5.17), not too clearly for those who are not sensitive to the niceties of participial agreement in Latin, that Aeneas, forced to leave Troy, settled on this island in the Adriatic. Dictys' passage reads as follows:

Aeneas orat uti secum Antenorem regno exagerent. Quae postquam praeverso de se nuntio Antenori cognita sunt, regrediens ad Troiam inperfecto negotio aditu prohibetur. Ita coactus cum omni patrimonio ab Troia navigat. Cf. the note on this passage in Léopold Constans *Le Roman de Troie* (Paris, Firmin-Didot, 1909) V 19f.

55. A persistent mediaeval tradition attributed the death of Achilles to his betrayal by Paris in the temple of Apollo when Achilles went there unattended to arrange for his marriage with Polyxena. Cf. Sir James George Frazer *Apollodorus, the Library* (London, Heinemann, Loeb Classical Library, 1921) II 215, translator's note; and Landor's version of this story, p. 60.

56. Cf. L. Constans and E. Faral *Le Roman de Troie en Prose* (Paris, Champion, 1922) I 110 lines 53-55.

57. 4.9.

58. Chapter xxiv.

59. Chapter xxxiii.

60. For references to Troilus in ancient literature see Frazer, *op. cit.* (see note 55) II note 3 on pp. 201-203.

61. For the story in the versions of Benoit, Boccaccio, and Chaucer cf. R. K. Gordon *The Story of Troilus* (London, Dent and Sons, 1934).

62. For a brief sketch of Troy's mediaeval legend cf. *The Encyclopaedia Britannica* (11th edition), "Troy and Troad," XXVII 317f.

63. After an interval of many centuries a new edition of Guido's work recently has appeared under the auspices of The Medieval Academy of America, edited by Nathaniel E. Griffin (Harvard University Press, 1936).

64. The following delightful volumes by Douglas Bush will be found highly rewarding by readers interested in the tradition of classical mythology: *Mythology and the Renaissance Tradition in English Poetry* (Minneapolis, University of Minnesota Press, 1932), and *Mythology and the Romantic Tradition in English Poetry* (Cambridge, Harvard University Press, 1937).

65. Cf. John S. P. Tatlock "The Siege of Troy in Elizabethan Literature, especially in Shakespeare and Heywood," *Publications, Modern Language Association* XXX (1915) 680.

66. Cf. Bush *Mythology and the Romantic Tradition* 62f.

67. Quintus of Smyrna 10.259-331, 411-489; Apollodorus 3.12.6.

68. Cf. Homer *Odyssey* 4.271-289; Tryphiodorus 463-490.

69. Cf. Post, *op. cit.* (see note 3 in chapter ii) 165, 167, 181.

70. 6.56.

71. Published in *Songs and Satires* (New York, Macmillan, 1916).

72. See ends of second, third, and fourth acts.

73. Published in *Heavens and Earth* (New York, Henry Holt, 1920).

74. Cf. Alexander Cowie "The New Heroine's Code for Virtue," *The American Scholar* IV 2 (1935) 190-202.

# Notes to Chapter IV

1. 7.5.

2. *Cena* 29.

3. J. Overbeck *Die antiken Schriftquellen zur Geschichte der bildenden Künste bei den Griechen* (Leipzig, Engelmann, 1868), 382. All references to this book are to the number of the selection and not to the page.

4. *Ibid.* 612 (Pausanias 5.19.2).

5. 10.25-27.

6. Cf. W. R. Paton *The Greek Anthology* (London, Heinemann, Loeb Classical Library) V (1918) 248f. (book 16, selection 150) and editor's note.

7. *Aeneid* 2.785-788.

8. Cf. Mary H. Swindler *Ancient Painting from the Earliest Times to the Period of Christian Art* (New Haven, Yale University Press, 1929) 199f.; and J. G. Frazer *Pausanias's Description of Greece* (London, Macmillan, 1898) V, facing p. 360.

9. Overbeck, *op. cit.* (see note 3) 1054 (Pausanias 10.15.2).

10. *Ibid.* 1060 (Pausanias 1.22.6).

11. Pausanias 5.11.6. Cf. Swindler, *op. cit.* 221.

12. Overbeck, *op. cit.* 1667-1675. See p. 128 for reference to Vincent's painting of this story.

13. *Ibid.* 1699.

14. *Ibid.* 2125.

15. Athenaeus 5.207c-d.

16. Cf. Louis E. Lord "The Judgment of Paris on Etruscan Mirrors" *American Journal of Archaeology* XLI (1937) 602-606. The monumental work on Etruscan mirrors is that of Eduard Gerhard *Etruskische Spiegel* (Berlin, Reimer, 1840-1897).

17. Cf. Karl Lehmann-Hartleben "Two Roman Silver Jugs" *American Journal of Archaeology* XLII (1938) 82-105.

18. Swindler, *op. cit.* (see note 8) 242 and illustration 390.

19. *Ibid.* 253f.

20. *Ibid.* 256f. and illustration 431.

21. *Ibid.* 373 and illustration 581.

22. *Ibid.* 286f. and illustration 459; R. Engelmann, tr. by W. Anderson *Pictorial Atlas to Homer's Iliad and Odyssey* (London, Grevel, 1892): *Iliad* 4.10. In this and future references to this book the first figure refers to the plate and the second to the illustration.

23. Ludwig Curtius *Die Wandmalerei Pompejis* (Leipzig, Seeman, 1929): illustrations 137, 138.

24. Swindler, *op. cit.* 373 and illustration 578; Engelmann-Anderson, *op. cit.* (see note 22): *Odyssey* 5.33.

25. Two fragmentary mosaics found at Pompeii also portray the quarrel of Agamemnon and Achilles related in the first book of the *Iliad*. Cf. Engelmann-Anderson, *op. cit.* (see note 22): *Iliad* 3.9.

26. *Aeneid* 6.518f.

27. Swindler, *op. cit.* (see note 8) 381.

28. Cf. Jane E. Harrison "The Judgment of Paris. Two Unpublished Vases in the Graeco-Etruscan Museum at Florence" *Journal of Hellenic Studies* VII (1886) 196-219. Miss Harrison also mentions here three vases bearing this story in Copenhagen, two in the Louvre, one in the National Museum at Naples, and two in

Palermo. Chapter xviii of Percy Gardner's *The Principles of Greek Art* (New York, Macmillan, 1914) is devoted to a study of this one story in the history of Greek ceramics. Several vases not referred to in the present chapter are discussed by Gardner.

29. J. C. Hoppin *A Handbook of Attic Red-Figured Vases* (Cambridge, Harvard University Press, 1919) II 42f.

30. This, too, is a common theme on vases. Especially noteworthy is the beautiful *cotyle* (two-handled cup) in the Boston Museum of Fine Arts. Cf. Hoppin, *op. cit.* II 52f.

31. Gisela M. A. Richter *Handbook of the Classical Collection* (New York, The Metropolitan Museum of Art, 1927) 130f.; same author, *op. cit.* (see note 57) I 101-103 and II plate 77.

32. J. C. Hoppin *A Handbook of Greek Black-Figured Vases* (Paris, Champion, 1924) 150-155.

33. For examples cf. Gardner, *op. cit.* (see note 28) 275f. and Salomon Reinach *Répertoire des Vases peints grecs et étrusques* (Paris, Leroux, 1899-1900, 2 v.) II 97.

34. Hoppin, *op. cit.* (see note 29) II 80f.; Engelmann-Anderson, *op. cit.: Iliad* 4.11; Gardner, *op. cit.* (see note 28) 270-273.

35. Hoppin, *op. cit.* (see note 29) II 80f.; Engelmann-Anderson, *op. cit.* (see note 22): *Iliad* 10.50.

36. Engelmann-Anderson, *op. cit.: Iliad* 8.42. The caption under this figure has by mistake been exchanged with that of plate 6, illustration 23, in the work cited.

37. *Ibid. Iliad* 6.23. As explained in the preceding note, the caption is attached to the wrong picture. Hoppin, *op. cit.* (see note 29) I 244f.

38. J. D. Beazley "Fragment of a Vase at Oxford and the Painter of the Tyszkiewicz Crater in Boston," *American Journal of Archaeology* XX (1916), figs. 2 and 3 on 145f.; Hoppin, *op. cit.* (see note 29) II 143, item 20; and II 459, item 4.

39. *Eros and Psyche, March* 27-28 and *Iliad* 18.39-49. Cf. also Spenser *Faery Queen* 4.11.48-51 and Bush *Mythology and the Romantic Tradition* (see note 63 of chapter iii) note 9 on p. 435.

40. Richter, *op. cit.* (see note 57) I 175-178 and plates 143, 144, 176 in Volume II.

41. Hoppin, *op. cit.* (see note 29) I 126, item 30.

42. Cf. Richter, *op. cit.* (see note 31) 94f.

43. Hoppin, *op. cit.* (see note 29) I 140f. item 101; Engelmann-Anderson, *op. cit.* (see note 22): *Iliad* 20.108.

44. Richter, *op. cit.* (see note 57) I 38f. and note 3 on p. 38; and plates 16, 172 in Volume II.

45. H. N. Fowler and J. R. Wheeler *A Handbook of Greek Archaeology* (New York, American Book Co., 1909) 516 f. and fig. 402.

46. See pp. 27, 47. Gardner, *op. cit.* (see note 28) 199f. discusses a vase bearing this story. Cf. also J. D. Beazley *Attic Red-Figured Vases in American Museums* (Cambridge, Harvard University Press, 1918) 38, 48, 65, 79, 145.

47. *Aeneid* 2.15.

48. Engelmann-Anderson, *op. cit.* (see note 22): *Odyssey* 5.32.

49. Hoppin, *op. cit.* (see note 32) 440f.

50. Hoppin, *op. cit.* (see note 29) II 125, item 4.

51. *Ibid.* II 236f., item 32; Engelmann-Anderson, *op. cit.: Odyssey* 10.56.

52. E. A. Gardner "A Lecythus from Eretria with the Death of Priam" *Journal of Hellenic Studies* XIV (1894) 170-185. Cf. also Richter, *op. cit.* (see note 57) I 41-43.

53. Hoppin, *op. cit.* (see note 32) 258f.

54. *Ibid.* 297, item 99.

55. Reinach, *op. cit.* (see note 33), publishes at least seven black-figured vases portraying the flight of Aeneas with his father, child, and wife, though the child is lacking in one of these (II 108.9; 110; 116.4; 116.5; 273; 274; 333). Two other vases of Reinach's collection (II 108.7; 332) probably have the same story on them, too.

56. Arthur Fairbanks *Athenian Lekythoi* (New York, Macmillan, 1907) 247f.

57. In addition to the volumes of Hoppin already cited there are, among others, the following: Reinach *Répertoire* (see note 33); Adolf Furtwängler and K. Reichhold *Griechische Vasenmalerei* (München, Bruckmann, 1904-1932); H. B. Walters *History of Ancient Pottery* (New York, Scribner's Sons, and London, Murray, 1905, 2 v.), especially pp. 119-138; L. D. Caskey *Attic Vase Paintings in the Museum of Fine Arts, Boston* (London, H. Milford, Oxford University Press, 1931); Gisela M. A. Richter *Red-figured Athenian Vases in the Metropolitan Museum of Art* (New Haven, Yale University Press, 1936, 2 v.); and J. D. Beazley, *Attic Red-figure Vase Painters* (Oxford, Clarendon Press, 1942) 978-986.

58. Paul Schubring *Cassoni* (Leipzig, Hiersemann, 1915, 2 v.), items 227-239 respectively. There is also a supplement of the same title and published by the same author and publisher (1923).

59. *Op. cit.*, item 168. Van Marle, *op. cit.* (see note 62) X 570 gives a different opinion regarding this panel.

60. Schubring, *Supplement,* item 930.

61. *Ibid.,* item 956. Cf. also Tancred Borenius "Unpublished Cassone Panels" *Burlington Magazine* XL (1922) 74f.

62. *Op. cit.,* item 69. Cf. also Raimond Van Marle *The Development of the Italian Schools of Painting* (The Hague, Nijhoff, 1923-1938, 19 volumes) VII 333 (Schubring 648), X 198 (Schubring 88), X 199-201 (Schubring 165), X 570 (Schubring 166), X 571 (Schubring 163), X 572 (Schubring 179), XII 410, XIII 264 (Schubring, *Supplement* 923), XVI 426 (Schubring 480). *Cassone* 88 of Schubring, which he assigns to Florence of about the year 1430 shows the goddesses dressed as Florentine noble ladies; likewise his *cassoni* 163, 166, and 179 (both the latter assigned to the "Paris-Master"). But in Schubring's *cassone* 648, assigned to a Veronese artist of about the year 1450, the goddesses are nude; likewise his *cassone* 165. Then Schubring's *cassone* 480, assigned to an artist of Bologna of the end of the fifteenth century, has Aphrodite nude, but the other two goddesses dressed.

Finally, Schubring's *cassone* 69, assigned to Florence of about the year 1470, has the goddesses draped.

63. They will be found reproduced respectively in Schubring, *op. cit.* 504 and 508, 505 (All three preceding will be found in Van Marle XVI 520), 506, 507, 69, 510, 144, 222. *Cassoni* 504 and 505 are in contemporary costume. In *cassone* 144 the warriors are clothed in contemporary armor, and the market place of Troy resembles the style of the Loggia dei Lanzi at Florence.

64. Cf. Van Marle, *op. cit.* XIII 236; XIII 255 (Schubring 393, 394); X 552; XIII 262 respectively for this and the following three themes.

65. Van Marle, *op. cit.* XVIII 373, XI 617, XVI 464.

66. A reproduction of the last of these may be seen in *Bryan's Dictionary of Painters and Engravers* (revised edition of Williamson, London, G. Bell and Sons, 5 v.) in connection with the account regarding the artist, II (1914) opposite 244.

67. Reproduced in Lady Dilke *French Painters of the Eighteenth Century* (London, G. Bell and Sons, 1899) plate 50.

68. Schubring *Supplement* (see note 58), item 937. Cf. also George H. Edgell *A History of Sienese Painting* (New York, The Dial Press, 1932), fig. 356. Other versions of the story will be found in Van Marle, *op. cit.* X 570 (Schubring 167); 571 (Schubring 164); XVI 257 (Schubring *Supplement* 937); 388 (Schubring 476). Schubring's *cassoni* 167, 164, 476 depict forcible abductions with Helen in distress, and their setting of costume and architectural background is of the Renaissance.

69. Reproduced in L. Dimier *French Painting in the Sixteenth Century* (London, Duckworth and Co., New York, Scribner's, 1904), plate facing 116.

70. Reproduced in *Life Magazine,* July 29, 1940.

71. Pompeo Molmenti *Tiepolo, La Villa Valmarana* (Venice, F. Ongania, 1928), plates 8 and 9.

72. Pompeo Molmenti *Tiepolo, la Vie et l'Oeuvre du Peintre* (Paris, Hachette, 1911, translation of H. L. De Perera), plate 148.

73. *Ibid.,* plate 202.

74. Schubring, *op. cit.,* plate 166, item 789.

75. Heinrich Göbel *Wandteppiche* III 2 (Berlin, Brandus, 1934), fig. 176a.

76. *Göbel, op. cit.* II 2 (*Die romanischen Länder* [Leipzig, Klinkhardt und Biermann, 1928]), figs. 268, 269.

77. *Ibid.,* fig. 438.

78. *Ibid.,* fig. 271. This tapestry is incorrectly named by the author as depicting Hector and Anchises. The book has other mistakes, too.

79. *Ibid.,* fig. 150.

80. *Ibid.,* fig. 173. Cf. also fig. 177 for the same subject.

81. *Ibid.,* fig. 242.

82. *Ibid.,* II 1.200.

83. Cf. Alfred M. Frankfurter "Gothic Trojan War Tapestries" *International Studio* XCII (1929) 35-40; and "The Arrival of Hercules and Jason at Troy" *Bulletin of the Milwaukee Art Institute* 9 (1934) 1f.

84. Cf. H. C. Marillier "The Tapestries of the Painted Chamber; The 'Great History of Troy'" *Burlington Magazine* XLVI (1925) 35-42.

85. Reproduced in W. G. Thomson *A History of Tapestry* (New York, Putnam's Sons, 1906), facing 142; and in part in *The Encyclopaedia Britannica* (11th edition), "Tapestry," XXVI 404 in figs. 14 and 15 of plate 3. For Foucquet's design of this hanging cf. *ibid.*, fig. 13.

86. Reproduced in Heinrich Göbel *Tapestries of the Lowlands,* translated by Robert West (New York, Brentano's, 1924), figs. 220 and 221. For another Lowland tapestry of a later date cf. that of the burning of Troy made at Delft in 1622, *ibid.*, fig. 494.

87. Göbel, *op. cit.* (see note 75) III 2. fig. 123b.

88. Phyllis Ackerman *Tapestry, the Mirror of Civilization* (Oxford University Press, 1933) 189 and plate 27.

89. Cf. S. E. Morison *The Ancient Classics in a Modern Democracy* (Oxford University Press, N. Y., 1939) 22f.

90. Reproduced in Richard Cantinelli *Jacques-Louis David* (Paris, G. Van Oest, 1930) plate I.

91. Reproduced in Henry Lapauze *Ingres, Sa Vie et son Oeuvre* (Paris, Georges Petit, 1911) 101.

92. *Ibid.* 513.

93. See page 38.

94. For these and further contributions of Wedgwood and Flaxman in this field the following books may be consulted: T. Piroli *The Iliad of Homer Engraved from the Compositions of John Flaxman* (London, Longman, Hurst, Rees and Orme, 1805); Eliza Meteyard *Wedgwood and His Works* (London, Bell and Daldy, 1873); W. G. Constable *John Flaxman* (London, University of London Press, 1927).

95. 459-461.

96. With all its long tradition in literature and the arts the Trojan horse has also had a curious linguistic tradition. The homely association of it and its burden of warriors with a sow laden with her young gave rise in the popular mind to the word *troja* meaning *sow* in Italian, to the French *truie* with the same meaning, to the Spanish *troya* meaning *procuress* or *midwife,* and to the Sardinian *troyu* meaning *dirty.*

97. Reproduced in Max Schmid *Max Klinger* (Leipzig, Velhagen und Klasing, 1926) 75.

98. Reproduced in A. R. H. Moncrieff *Classic Myth and Legend* (New York, W. H. Wise and Co., 1934) facing 224.

99. Reproduced in René Huyghe *Histoire de l'Art contemporain. La Peinture* (Paris, Félix Alcan, 1934) 64 and illustration 64.

100. *Ibid.,* illustration 388 on p. 298.

# Notes to Chapter V

1. 5.19.1-8.

2. 5.25.8-10. Overbeck, *op. cit.* (see note 3 to chapter iv) 425.

3. Pausanias 5.22.2-3. Overbeck, *op. cit.* 862.

4. Pausanias 3.18.12.

5. 1.23.8. Overbeck, *op. cit.* 884-888.

6. Swindler, *op. cit.* (see note 8 to chapter iv) 219f. Cf. also Edward Robinson *Museum of Fine Arts, Boston: Catalogue of Casts, Part III* (Boston, Houghton Mifflin, 1892) 217-219.

7. Pausanias 2.17.3. Overbeck, *op. cit.* 1014.

8. 36.26. Overbeck, *op. cit.* 1175.

9. Maxime Collignon *Histoire de la Sculpture grecque* (Paris, Firmin-Didot, 1892-1897, 2 v.) I 184-188 and illustration 87.

10. A fragmentary relief of the fourth century B.C. in the Metropolitan Museum is supposed to be another replica of this well-known subject. The same subject is engraved on one of this Museum's Etruscan mirrors.

11. Adolf Furtwängler and H. L. Urlichs *Greek and Roman Sculpture* (London, J. M. Dent and Sons, 1914, translated by Horace Taylor) 155-157 and plate 41.

12. Walther Amelung *Die Sculpturen des Vaticanischen Museums* (Berlin, Georg Reimer, 1908) II (Tafeln), plates 13 and 7.54.

13. Furtwängler-Urlichs, *op. cit.* 158-163 and plate 42.

14. Engelmann-Anderson, *op. cit.* (see note 22 to chapter iv) *Iliad* 19.109.

15. George H. Chase *Greek and Roman Sculpture in American Collections* (Cambridge, Harvard University Press, 1924) 149 and illustration 177.

16. 36.37.

17. *Childe Harold* 4.160.

18. Daremberg-Saglio *Dictionnaire des Antiquités grecques et romaines* (Paris, Hachette, 1900), "Iliacae."

19. Cf. L. D. Caskey *Museum of Fine Arts, Boston. Catalogue of Greek and Roman Sculpture* (Cambridge, Harvard University Press, 1925) 115-117.

20. Arthur H. Smith *A Guide to the Department of Greek and Roman Antiquities in the British Museum*[5] (London, British Museum, 1920) 75f.; Engelmann-Anderson, *op. cit.* (see note 22 to chapter iv), *Iliad* 1.2.

21. H. B. Walters *Catalogue of the Engraved Gems and Cameos, Greek, Etruscan and Roman in the British Museum* (London, 1926), plate 32.3190.

22. Adolf Furtwängler *Die antiken Gemmen* (Leipzig, Giesecke und Devrient, 1900, 3 v.) I, plate 52.7.

23. Gisela M. A. Richter *Catalogue of Engraved Gems of the Classical Style, Metropolitan Museum of Art* (New York, 1920), plate 81.409.

24. *Ibid.* 72.326. On some gems Troilus is accompanied by Polyxena. Cf. Furtwängler, *op. cit.* (see note 22) 58.7 (a cameo) and 63.44, though in neither case is the attribution entirely certain.

25. Cf. Gisela M. A. Richter *Handbook of the Etruscan Collection* (New York, The Metropolitan Museum of Art, 1940) 31.

26. Richter, *op. cit.* (see note 23) 29.84.

27. Furtwängler, *op. cit.* (see note 22) 23.54.

28. *Ibid.* 23.56.

29. Walters, *op. cit.* (see note 21) 14.965 and 966.

30. *Ibid.* 3203.

31. Engelmann-Anderson, *op. cit.* (see note 22 to chapter iv), *Iliad* 12.69.

32. *Ibid. Iliad* 12.70.

33. Richter, *op. cit.* (see note 25) 31 and fig. 95.

34. Furtwängler, *op. cit.* (see note 22) 38.6. Cf. also August Baumeister *Denkmäler des klassischen Altertums* (München, R. Oldenbourg, 1885-1888) I 742, illustration 794.

35. Walters, *op. cit.* (see note 21) 11.673; Furtwängler, *op. cit.* (see note 22) 64.30.

36. Richard Förster "Laokoon-Denkmäler und-Inschriften," *J. A. I.* VI (1891) 177-196, and "Noch Zwei Laokoondenkmäler," *J. A. I.* IX (1894) 43-50. Margarete Bieber *Laocoön. The Influence of the Group Since Its Rediscovery* (New York, Columbia University Press, 1942).

37. Walters, *op. cit.* (see note 21) 24.1942.

38. Richter, *op. cit.* (see note 23) 82.417.

39. Walters, *op. cit.* (see note 21) 3206.

40. Furtwängler, *op. cit.* (see note 22) 20.5.

41. *Ibid.* 27.55.

42. *Ibid.* 30.61.

43. Walters, *op. cit.* (see note 21) 24.1948-1950.

44. For a list of the seats of important collections of coins, public and private, see Karl Sittl *Archäologie der Kunst* (München, Beck, 1895) 865-872.

45. Barclay V. Head *Historia Numorum* (Oxford, Clarendon Press, 1911) 214.

46. Barclay V. Head *Catalogue of Greek Coins. Macedonia, etc.* (London, British Museum, 1879) 41f.

47. Head, *op. cit.* (see note 45) 167.

48. *Verrine Orations* 2.4.33.

49. Reginald S. Poole *Catalogue of Greek Coins. Sicily* (London, British Museum, 1876) 137.59 and 137.65.

50. H. A. Grueber *Coins of the Roman Republic in the British Museum* (London, British Museum, 1910, 3 v.) II 469.31-35.

51. *Ibid.* I 579.4257-4258.

52. Harold Mattingly *Coins of the Roman Empire in the British Museum* (London, British Museum, 1923-1940, 4 v.) III 141.31; same author and Edward A. Sydenham *The Roman Imperial Coinage* (London, Spink and Son, 1923-1938, 5 v.) II 302f., 309.801.

53. Mattingly, *op. cit.* (see note 52) IV 36.237; Mattingly and Sydenham, *op. cit.* III 37.91.

54. *Ibid.* III 109.615 and 111.627; Mattingly, *op. cit.* (see note 52) IV 203.1264 and 207.1292.

55. Warwick Wroth *Catalogue of the Greek Coins of Troas, Aeolis, and Lesbos* (London, British Museum, 1894) 60.28.

56. *Ibid.* 59.20.

57. *Ibid.* 51.29.

58. *Ibid.* 85.38.

59. L. Forrer *The Weber Collection* (London, Spink and Son, 1922-1929) III (part 2) 521.7132.

60. Head, *op. cit.* (see note 45) 510; Warwick Wroth *Catalogue of Greek Coins. Pontus, Paphlagonia, Bithynia, and the Kingdom of Bosporus* (London, British Museum, 1889) 114.37.

61. Head, *op. cit.* (see note 45) 682; same author *Catalogue of the Greek Coins of Phrygia* (London, British Museum, 1906) lxxxvii and 345.14.

62. Percy Gardner *Catalogue of Greek Coins. Peloponnesus* (London, British Museum, 1887) 28.44.

63. George F. Hill *Catalogue of the Greek Coins of Phoenicia* (London, British Museum, 1910) lviii and 84.213.

64. Head, *op. cit.* (see note 45) 547, 549, 733, 862.

65. George F. Hill *Catalogue of the Greek Coins of Lycaonia, Isauria, and Cilicia* (London, British Museum, 1900) 205.223.

66. For other representations of Hector on coins see Wroth, *op. cit.* (see note 55) 64.49; 65.56; 69.83; 70.88, 90-92; 66.63, 64. The association of Rome with Troy is effected in one instance by the presence of a wolf and the twins Romulus and Remus on the face of the coin. See Wroth 60.24.

67. *Ibid.* 70.92.

68. *Ibid.* 66.61,62. Cf. also 71.100.

69. *Ibid.* 68.75. Cf. *Iliad* 16.862f.

70. *Ibid.* 60; 64.50, 51; 67.69.

71. See the indices of Barclay V. Head *Catalogue of the Greek Coins of Ionia* (London, British Museum, 1892); of Warwick Wroth *Catalogue of the Greek Coins of Crete and the Aegean Islands* (London, British Museum, 1886); and of Wroth, *op. cit.* (see note 60).

72. Wroth, *op. cit.* (see note 55) 60.27. Cf. also 51.28 and 64.51.

73. The second of these reliefs is reproduced in Count Cicognara *The Works of Antonio Canova in Sculpture and Modelling* (London, Chatto, 1876), plate following p. 70.

74. *Ibid.* 43 and two plates following p. 42.

75. *On the Bust of Helen by Canova.*

76. J. M. Thiele *Thorwaldsen and His Works* (New York, J. G. Unnevehr, 1869, translated by P. C. Sinding) I plate 36 and III plate 96. For other Trojan subjects cf. I 5, 17; II 87; III 16, 40, 93, 94, 95, 97, 98, 99.

77. Two of the preceding reliefs are reproduced in Eugene Plon *Thorvaldsen, His Life and Works* (Boston, Roberts Brothers, 1874, translated from French by I. M. Luyster), as follows: *The Arms of Achilles* 228; *Priam Beseeching Achilles* 192.

78. *Helen of Troy* 5.36, 37. Cf. also Thiele, *op. cit.* (see note 76) III 98.

79. Reproduced in Carl Laurin, Emil Hannover, Jens Thiis *Scandinavian Art* (London, H. Milford, and Oxford University Press, 1922) 409.

80. *Odyssey* 7.114- 131.

81. In the report in *The Studio* (London) XVIII (1900) 285-288 the work of these two young artists as well as two other versions of the same subject may be seen.

82. Chandler R. Post *A History of European and American Sculpture from the Early Christian Period to the Present Day* (Cambridge, Harvard University Press, 1921) II facing 266.

## Notes to Chapter VI

1. Cf. *The Greek Tradition* edited by George Boas (Baltimore, The Johns Hopkins University Press, 1939), chapter on "The Beginnings of Italian Opera" by Lubov Keefer, 91-135.

2. General reference books in the field of opera are:
François H. J. Blaze *L'opéra-italien de 1548 à 1856* (Paris, Castil-Blaze, 1856);
Carlo Dassori *Opere e operisti (Dizionario lirico universale 1541-1902)* (Genova, R. Istituto Sordomuti, 1903);
John Towers *Dictionary-Catalogue of Operas and Operettas* (Morgantown, West Virginia, Acme Publishing Co., 1910);
Alfred Loewenberg *Annals of Opera 1597-1940* (Cambridge, W. Heffer and Sons, Ltd., 1943).

3. Convenient handbooks for brief references to the commoner operas are:
W. L. Hubbard *The American History and Encyclopedia of Music* (Toledo, Irving Squire, 1908): *Operas* I, II;
Leo Melitz *The Opera Goers' Complete Guide* (New York, Dodd, Mead, 1909, translation of Richard Salinger);
F. H. Martens *A Thousand and One Nights of Opera* (New York, Appleton, 1926).
Waldemar Rieck *Opera Plots* (New York, Public Library, 1927);
Oscar Thompson *The International Cyclopedia of Music and Musicians* (New York, Dodd, Mead, 1939).

4. See Siegfried Kracauer *Orpheus in Paris,* translation of David and Mosbacher (New York, Knopf, 1938), chapter ix.

# INDEX

# INDEX

# INDEX

# INDEX

192

# INDEX

# INDEX

This book has been printed from Caslon and
Forum types on Worthy Text for the
University of Pittsburgh Press
by Davis & Warde, Inc.,
Pittsburgh